D0962175

THE MOST
POWERFUL
WOMAN
IN THE ROOM
IS YOU

THE MOST POWERFUL WOMAN IN THE ROOM IS YOU

COMMAND AN AUDIENCE AND SELL YOUR WAY TO SUCCESS

LYDIA FENET

GALLERY BOOKS

New York   London   Toronto   Sydney   New Delhi

Gallery Books
An Imprint of Simon & Schuster, Inc.
1230 Avenue of the Americas
New York, NY 10020

First Gallery Books hardcover edition 2019

GALLERY BOOKS and colophon are registered trademarks of Simon & Schuster, Inc.

For information about special discounts for bulk purchases,
please contact Simon & Schuster Special Sales at 1-866-506-1949
or business@simonandschuster.com.

The Simon & Schuster Speakers Bureau can bring authors to your live event.
For more information or to book an event, contact the Simon & Schuster Speakers Bureau
at 866-248-3049 or visit our website at www.simonspeakers.com.

Manufactured in the United States of America

1 3 5 7 9 10 8 6 4 2

Library of Congress Cataloging-in-Publication Data has been applied for.

ISBN 978-1-9821-0113-8
ISBN 978-1-9821-0115-2 (ebook)

For Mom and Dad, who taught me everything I know.
Your love has provided a safety net that allows me
to reach higher and higher without a fear of falling.
No one has ever been given more loving and
unconditional support than I have by you.
Thank you for everything. I love you.

For Chris, the best husband, father, and friend
I could have asked for in life.
You are my rock, and I could not
have done this without you.
I love you.

For Beatrice, Henry, and Eloise.
There are no words to describe my love for you.
I will love you for eternity.

For Charles, Andrew, and Hilary,
who pushed me to run faster and jump higher.
You are my inspiration and my motivation.

CONTENTS

Your Time Is Now

You were curious, right?

That's why you picked up this book.

Somewhere deep down you believe that you have a voice that needs to be heard, that you have what it takes to not only succeed but also excel in life. Maybe you feel this way because it was what your parents or teachers told you. Or maybe you believe it despite what people have been telling you all along. All you know is that you are ready. Ready to make your voice heard and ready to reach the goals that you see in front of you.

What I want you to know is that you are the only person who can change the course of your life. You *can* be whatever you want to be and you *can* do whatever you want to do. But you will need to learn how to use the voice inside you to sell your way to the life that you want.

To excel in life will take commitment, hard work, and dedication. You will need to create a road map that keeps you focused on what you want to achieve. There will be rejection and failure along the way—and you may worry those failures will define you. Trust that you will grow stronger with each failure. In time you will understand why you needed to go through those moments in order to be prepared for even more challenging life experiences. And most importantly, you will pass your knowledge along to others who are just starting on their journey or need a little motivation so that you will bring along a network of people who are inspired by you and hold you accountable for the goals that you are setting. And you will do this for them.

I know this because I am you. Twenty years ago I would have walked into a bookstore and picked up this book because deep down I always knew that I wanted to live an extraordinary life. I always believed that I had what it took to succeed, but I didn't yet know what that meant or how I would get there. As you will read in this book, it took me many years working tirelessly, learning lessons the hard way, utilizing the network that I was always growing, taking risks, and trying again. I took every opportunity that presented itself and found a way to maximize it. There are no shortcuts in life, but my hope is that you will read this book and achieve your goals in the shortest time possible for you. And then set new, higher goals and keep reaching.

I am writing this book to tell you anything in life is possible if you see roadblocks as hurdles instead of barriers. There is nothing you cannot do if you put your mind to it and commit to following through. If I can find time to write a book on deadline while juggling the schedules of three children, spending time with my husband, and managing a full-time career and a night job as a charity auctioneer, you can achieve your dreams too.

Nobody picks up a book titled *The Most Powerful Woman in the Room Is You* unless that is who she wants to be. I want this book to change your life. I want it to inspire you, motivate you, and push you to be the best you can be—and to raise up other people along with you while you do it.

The Most Powerful Woman in the Room is me.

But most importantly, the Most Powerful Woman in the Room is you too.

THE MOST
POWERFUL
WOMAN
IN THE
ROOM . . .

1

uses the strike method

" Lydia, you are on in two minutes," says the stagehand dressed head to toe in black, sporting a headset while standing right next to me.

I take a deep breath and look down at my pile of notes, twisting the top of my gavel over and over in my right hand. Adrenaline starts to course through my veins as I stare out from the darkness of backstage at the faces of 1,000 audience members staring up at a perfectly edited video explaining the mission of the charity.

"Lydia, you are on in thirty seconds."

He hands me the microphone. I close my eyes and my mind becomes laser-focused on the perfect opening line. So much is at stake in the first five seconds of an auction. If I don't come up with something dynamic enough to hold the attention of the audience, within seconds the noise from 1,000 guests will completely overpower the room, and I might as well join someone at the table for a drink because no one will be listening to me.

"Lydia, stand by for the Voice of God announcement," he said, referring to the man who announces the next speaker from behind the stage curtain. "Go in 5, 4 . . ."

I walk quickly from the wings onto the stage, adjusting my eyes to the bright lighting and surveying the crowd. I have chosen my dress carefully: a power red that is eye-catching enough to attract attention but also shows that I mean business. My long brown hair is curled to show that I put in the effort, but having three small children running around at home means that I rarely have time for Drybar before going onstage in the evening.

"3, 2, 1 . . ."

"Please welcome Lydia Fenet, managing director and lead benefit auctioneer for Christie's Auction House!"

I stride purposefully toward the podium, take a couple of seconds to spread my notes across it, pausing just long enough to make the crowd look up to figure out why I am not talking.

CRACK, CRACK, CRACK. I slam down my gavel so forcefully that half the audience jumps in their seats.

I call it "the Strike."

The Strike has become my signature move. I never start an auction without it. A few times I have forgotten my gavel and had to improvise—an empty saltshaker, a jar of Kiehl's face cream from the goody bag at my chair, a tube of Laura Mercier lipstick. Other times the organization doesn't have a podium and I have had to use other things—the rail of a staircase, the top of a piano, a wooden block I found backstage. A frequent auction bidder once told me I should patent the gavel strike; there is little doubt who is leading the auction when bidders hear the repeated cracks of my gavel against the podium. Whatever it takes. I always start with the Strike. And once the gavel hits the podium, I never back down.

Years before I became an auctioneer, I had unknowingly used my earliest version of the Strike to gain an internship at Christie's.

My sophomore year in college, I applied for a European Studies program that allowed me to spend a semester of my junior year at Oxford University followed by a month traveling through France, Spain, and Italy studying art. Prior to that semester, my exposure to art was probably similar to what most people are exposed to in their lives: a picture of van Gogh's *The Starry Night* in a textbook, a poster of Monet's *Water Lilies* purchased from a college bookstore, and, in my case, a lot of vacations spent being dragged around to museums by my parents while my siblings and I lobbied them to ditch the art in lieu of an ice-cream stand out front.

What I didn't realize when we were traipsing through the museums with my parents was that each painting had a story—in most cases, many stories—that elevated it from flat art on the wall to a dynamic, exciting masterpiece. When I was older and studying at Oxford, as we walked through the museums with our professor, she brought each piece to life by telling the story of the painter who created it, or how it was considered risqué at the time because of its subject matter, how the painting had fallen into the hands of one patron or another, and how it ultimately had ended up in that museum. I spent the semester enthralled as we visited museum after museum and studied masterpieces while balancing notebooks and pencils, trying to jot down every last comment. After finishing the semester and trying out every pasta bar in Italy, I immediately declared a second major in art history and spent the next year and a half cramming art history classes into my schedule.

It was toward the end of my time abroad that I stumbled upon an article in a magazine about women who worked in auction houses. Up until this time it had never occurred to me that there was a vibrant, energetic business element to the art world. I assumed that a person would just walk into an art gallery and buy whatever they wanted off the wall. Actually, I don't even think that I had ever given it a thought. Art, to me, was something that hung on the wall of a museum, not the wall of your house. The article focused on the glamour of a job in the auction world—the high stakes that specialists faced when they were tracking down a piece of art that had previously been considered lost or stolen, the amazing events that top clients around the world flew to New York and London to attend in advance of the big auctions, the international travel, the interfacing with the most powerful people in the world, the opportunity to see museum-quality art every day as part of your job. I was completely enthralled. The thought of working in a place where a rediscovered Leonardo da Vinci might be hanging on the wall one week and a Degas might be hanging on that same wall the following week seemed like a dream. After I did some basic research, it was clear that the two top auction houses in the world were Christie's and Sotheby's, so I sat down to write out a road map that would help me achieve my goal of securing an internship at one of them.

I spent the next couple of months researching the auction world and telling anyone who would listen that I was looking for an internship in that field. To me, telling anyone and everyone about my goals in life is the same thing as free marketing. You never know who might be able to help you along the way, so never be afraid to put it out there. Also, it serves another purpose: it holds you accountable. People will check in with you to see if you have made progress along the way. This doesn't mean that you should talk about something endlessly and leave it up to fate, but it never hurts to have additional networks engaged whenever possible. After telling everyone in the world about my interest in the auction world, I had a stroke of luck. Over Christmas that year, in what I like to think of as divine intervention, my father met a stylish young woman at a cocktail party who worked for Christie's. She was everything that the article said a woman who worked at Christie's would be—chic, well spoken, beautifully dressed; I like to believe that she was wearing an Hermès scarf, though I am sure I added that detail in to make for a better story. Over a glass of wine, she kindly handed over the golden ticket: the contact information for Mary Libby, the matriarch of Christie's who has run the internship program for over thirty years.

Now, if you are part of Generation Y or Z, a millennial, or whatever we have named the next generation, you might have a hard time understanding this part of the story. But, truth be told, there was a time when there was no caller ID (jaws off the floor, people). That's right. People had no idea who was calling them, so they had to pick up EVERY SINGLE TIME. Poor Mary Libby had no idea on that day when she picked up the phone and kindly (but firmly) explained that the internship program was full . . . that I wasn't going to take no for an answer.

Enter the Strike.

I began Grade A, Category 5 phone stalking. Every morning I would sit in my room and devise a script for what I wanted to say to Ms. Libby. I would write out my argument and counter-arguments on a single piece of paper in all caps and place the piece of paper in front of me. I would take a couple of deep breaths so that my voice wasn't shaking and dial Ms. Libby's number at Christie's. When she answered the phone, I would always start the call exactly the same way: "Ms. Libby, this is Lydia Fenet calling again, and I am certain that today is the day that we are going to find a way for me to intern at Christie's this summer." The first couple of days that I called, Ms. Libby would laugh and say something kind like, "Oh dear, unfortunately we still haven't been able to come up with a solution yet. I am afraid nothing has opened up."

After a few more days of getting nowhere, I amended my strategy. Instead of trying to have the same conversation over and over again, which inevitably ended up with Ms. Libby saying, "I'm afraid the answer is still no," I took a new approach. I wrote up a list of questions about why the internship program was capped at thirty people. My thought was that if I could find a flaw in the thirty-person cap for the intern program, I might have a chance at being the exception to the rule.

The next morning when I called, I greeted Ms. Libby as usual, and before she could give the obligatory "nothing yet," I quickly asked her why the program had to be capped at thirty people, especially given the fact that the internship was unpaid. I noted that it seemed like the departments in the company would always be happy to have an eager intern who was choosing to work for free. Ms. Libby revealed that the issue was that the interns took field trips to a number of museums every week, and there were a couple of trips that couldn't accommodate more than thirty people; therefore, they capped the program at thirty. And that was exactly what I needed to hear.

"What if," I asked, "I could do a modified internship where I didn't attend the museum trips where they could only fit thirty people? It would be better for the departments because I would be there all week without any afternoons off. And if, for example, one of your interns stayed out too late the night before [so irresponsible!] and called in sick, I could fill in their spot at the museum trip."

Ms. Libby didn't say yes. But for the first time she didn't say no.

An hour after I hung up, she called me back and told me that I couldn't attend every lecture or event because of space restraints, but I could do a modified internship and work in the business development department, where I could learn the auction vocabulary from the bottom up.

I could have been mopping the floors for all I cared. I wasn't going to squander the one chance that I had to fulfill my dream of working in the auction world. I moved to New York that summer and dressed exactly as the aforementioned article suggested. I donned my black suit and a scarf borrowed from my mom, and I marched into the front door of Christie's on Park Avenue ready to take over the company. It sounded incredibly glamorous to be working in the business development department, and I rode the elevator up to the top floor, ready to see my corner office overlooking Park Avenue.

In reality, I had a tiny little desk facing a wall next to which a pile of papers four feet tall was stacked with a note that said, "Please shred." And thus the story of my summer turned out to be less about Hermès scarves and more about shredding piles of paper and faxing, filing, and filling out reports about potential clients for my boss. Still, I loved being at Christie's—the energy around sale times, the world-class masterpieces hung over every available inch of every room, the resounding crack of the gavel hitting the podium at the end of the sale. I was determined to do everything asked of me and more. I showed up every day with a smile on my face, a scarf around my neck, and paper cuts all over my fingers. At the end of the summer, they offered me a job.

I was only a junior at the time, and heartbroken that I couldn't accept their offer because I had to go back to college to finish up my senior year. I knew I wanted to return to Christie's, so I stayed in touch with Ms. Libby and my internship supervisor that entire year. I set up another internship when I finished college—this time in the special events department, whose team I had always admired from afar during my internship of faxing and paper shredding. I started my internship in September 1999 with a three-month expectation. By December, I had interviewed for and secured a full-time job at Christie's.

Even at the earliest stage in my career, it was clear to me that preparation, focus, and hard work were important to achieving success in any aspect of my life. But what I understand after almost two decades of working at Christie's is that these three things are *crucial* if you want to be successful. It doesn't matter if you are a high school teacher who is regularly speaking to a group of students, a CEO of a tech start-up trying to raise seed funding, or an artist who is negotiating a commission; you need to find your version of the Strike to help you crush your sale. Now, for the average person, walking into a meeting and slamming down a wooden gavel isn't likely to win you anything but a confused look and possibly an invitation to exit the building. As an auctioneer, I get the immediate sense of empowerment from the Strike that I need in order to own a stage in a crowded room of guests who have had more than one cocktail. The gavel strike shows that I am the person in charge—that there is only one person who will be speaking for the next half an hour, and that person is me.

Your "Strike Method" needs to be something that feels authentic to you—something that you can use every time you walk into a room so that you feel confident and comfortable from the minute you engage with the people in front of you. I have spoken with professional athletes, world-renowned actors, and influential motivational speakers, and every single one of them describes an action or a motivating thought that helps them quiet their brain, center their thinking, and move forward from a place of strength. My gavel strike is something I do every time. I don't need to think about anything when I slam down the gavel because it is routine and eases my nerves immediately. After all, I have done it more than a thousand times at the point of writing this. Your Strike Method should give you a moment to gather your thoughts and provide those few seconds of clarity you need in order to launch into your pitch. For me, it is a gavel strike. For some, it will be an action like clasping their hands together or pressing their hands firmly on either side of a table. For others, it will be a single sentence that moves the conversation from pleasantries to serious business. Whatever it is, your Strike Method needs to make you feel like you are about to own whatever room you are in and you won't be leaving until everyone there knows it.

While the Strike is important for the moment that you begin your pitch, preparation for what happens immediately after the Strike is equally important. Have you ever been in a meeting when the person who is presenting is so nervous that their voice shakes when they begin to talk? Nine times out of ten it is because, in addition to the anxiety people feel about speaking in public, the person who is pitching hasn't thought about what they are going to say after they begin talking. Not only is it nerve-racking for the speaker, but it is also distracting for the people who are listening to the speaker. Instead of focusing on what that person is saying, everyone in the room is feeling uncomfortable because the person presenting feels uncomfortable.

The next time you are in a situation where you are in charge of selling, pitching, or speaking, make sure you have thought through your Strike and opening line so you come into the moment like a woman who knows what she wants and is going to tell you how she is going to get it. Find whatever motion or sentence will help focus your thinking and pull all your ideas together. Once you have figured out what that is, you can channel it into the moment to give you the confidence to present yourself in an authentic way. This will also help if the person or people in front of you are doing something distracting or unnerving; their performance will not unsettle you or catch you off guard. You will be able to deliver your Strike from a point of strength and let the momentum that you have created in that moment carry you forward into a well-thought-out presentation, speech, or discussion.

I find that if I start my auctions or meetings with this moment—a gavel strike in an auction room or a thoughtful, composed sentence in a boardroom—then the rest of my selling techniques (creating a human connection, positivity, humor, good old-fashioned persuasion, and a touch of charm) will guarantee the end result that I am looking for in a sale.

As I sat in my childhood bedroom dialing the number of the most prestigious auction house in the world at the age of nineteen, I had no idea that my first time using the Strike would set in motion the wheels that would lead me to a twenty-year career at Christie's. But since that call, I have relied on it time and again to make sure I am focused and ready anytime I want to feel in control of a situation in life or in business. So remember to use the Strike every time you go after something that you want. Because the more you practice, the easier it will be, and when it becomes second nature to you, you will be able to command a meeting, a pitch, a room, or maybe even Madison Square Garden from the minute you start selling. And that will make you the most powerful woman in any room.

their strike method

HOLLY DUNLAP

CEO, Stylindex and Makono

Last week I was fundraising, pitching to an audience of 425 potential investors at the Royal Institution. Before all pitches—even one-on-one meetings with potential investors—I think about Malawi.

If I want to accomplish my goals with my charity, Makono, in Malawi, I will need to make a boatload of cash. That thought motivates me to get into sales mode, pep up my energy, and "do it for the kids!"

On the other side of the coin, thinking about Malawi before the meetings also makes me calm, because I know that worrying about flopping a meeting is a first-world problem, and I'm just lucky to be alive, fundraising for those who don't have the privileges I was born into. Reminding myself that raising money for a good cause can make a big difference but knowing that it's actually not everything is what allows me to relax and do my best.

MEGHAN O'LEARY

US Olympic Rower
and World Championship Silver Medalist

Six boats perfectly lined up across the water separated by only a few meters, locked into the starting gate and waiting—there is nothing quite like the beginning of a race in rowing. The tension in the air is palpable, and all I can hear is the water lapping against the side of the boat. In my particular event (the women's double sculls), races are usually just over six and a half minutes long, leaving little to no time for error or indecision. You have to be precise from stroke one. First to sixth place is often separated by less than a second.

When the referee calls the two-minute warning, I take a couple of deep breaths to shake out any tension, relax my body, and put the blinders on. I close my eyes for just a few seconds to visualize the key points in the race and remind myself of the hard work I've put in to bring me here. With each breath out, I put away all other distractions. Finally, just before the call-over for the start, I slap my hands against my legs and place my hand on my boat partner's back in front of me to signal to her that "we're ready, we trust each other, let's do this." This is my Strike Method.

The key to a successful race is to be fully present and in tune with just that one thing ahead of you, which in that moment for me is the first stroke and then the next and then the one after that. In that moment it can't matter if I had a bad warm-up or took the best strokes I have ever taken; it is only about what kind of performance I can put down from meter 0 to 2,000 when the starting horn goes off.

THE MOST
POWERFUL
WOMAN
IN THE
ROOM . . .

2

sells as herself

For some people, selling is second nature. You know, the girl who convinces you to buy a pair of fabulous earrings when you aren't even sure you can pay rent. The woman who convinces you that you *must own* this cashmere sweater even though you live in South Florida and had never heard of cashmere before that moment. The woman who convinces you that your life is not complete without . . . fill in the blank.

Every one of us has encountered a natural-born salesperson at some point. The words tumble from their lips with such ease and grace that you believe everything they say. Even if you aren't born to sell, the good news is that you can still learn how to do it effectively. And with practice, you can excel in the same way as someone who comes by it naturally.

If you have ever seen an auction portrayed in a TV show or a movie, the characters might change, the drama surrounding the auction might change, but one thing is constant. The auctioneer is almost always a silver-haired British man with a posh British accent wearing a perfectly tailored tuxedo. The elegant man holds court over the auction by driving up the bidding with great skill until the very last auction lot of the sale. Inevitably, the dramatic scene ends with two bidders duking it out by bidding up to a truly astronomical sum, at which point the auctioneer gives a long pause before hammering down his gavel with a firm "SOLD!"

And when I first started at Christie's, this was the case almost 90 percent of the time.

I entered Christie's fresh out of college in 1999 at the age of twenty-one. I knew nothing about selling and even less about the world of auctioneering. It wasn't long into my first year at Christie's that I realized it was very much an old boys' club where art was sold based on long-standing relationships. Contracts were signed with a handshake, business was done over lunch, and it was often an old family friend of a senior executive who would dictate whether we won the business.

The lead auctioneer for Christie's at that time was an elegant, silver-haired British man who was known throughout the art and auction world for his ability to get an extra bid out of a bidder with an arch of his eyebrow. During our major evening sales, he stood at the rostrum selling museum-quality pieces of art—Picassos, Monets, Renoirs—to private clients. Bidding regularly hit millions of dollars for a single work of art—in the major evening sales, bidding would fly past $1 million and up to $50 million for a single piece.

I remember watching in awe as he took bids effortlessly during one auction. The first bid came from a man seated in the front row, the second from a lady in the back of the room, the third from a young woman nervously phone bidding with a top client who was calling from his home in Monaco (that was me). Watching him was like watching the conductor at a symphony or a football coach directing his team from the sidelines—I didn't know what it took to do his job, but his ease and command of the situation made it look effortless. I stood at the phone bank bidding on behalf of our client, never tiring of the auctioneer's performance. Never in a million years did I think that I would have the chance to stand behind a podium and slam down a gavel. Well, that's not entirely true. I have always dreamed big.

When I tell people that I am an auctioneer for Christie's, the first question they ask is, "Do you talk fast?" My reply? "I do talk A LOT, and quickly, but I am not selling livestock, so there is no need for the fast-talking cattle-auction style you see on TV." They are usually a little disappointed, but they still seem impressed that I am an auctioneer. The second question is inevitably, "What is the most expensive thing you have ever sold at auction?" This one always gives me pause. You know that silver-haired British gentleman I was just describing? The one elegantly bouncing bids off top clients in the saleroom selling Picassos and Monets?

That's not me.

I am a benefit auctioneer. Sometimes I sell art, but mostly I sell priceless experiences, one-of-a-kind moments with celebrities or vacations that people dream about their entire lives. Priceless but not like a Picasso. Priceless like the opportunity to have dinner with George Clooney. Or a singing lesson with Lady Gaga.

In my first year at Christie's, I worked in the special events department, which was responsible for fielding all requests for benefit auctions. Nonprofits from around the world would reach out to request the expertise of a Christie's benefit auctioneer to raise critical funds at their gala, and the events department would in turn reach out to the trained auctioneers and, based on level of skill and experience, pair them with the right benefit auction. As a courtesy to our top clients and a marketing tool for the company, Christie's trained benefit auctioneers for charity auctions around the world. Benefit auctioneers were sent out to the most prestigious galas dressed in black tie or a cocktail dress to take the stage to encourage guests to give additional money to the charity.

When I first started at Christie's, there wasn't a huge difference between art auctioneers and benefit auctioneers. Most art auctioneers simply took benefit auctions the way they took art auctions. Benefit auctioneers would choose to take auctions if they were available or if a top client had asked them to do it for his or her nonprofit. As far as I could tell in my early days at Christie's, the most glaring difference between art auctions and benefit auctions was the audience you faced in each auction setting.

During art auctions, clients are invited into the elegant salerooms of Christie's in New York, London, and Hong Kong. They walk into well-lit rooms with rows of perfectly spaced chairs facing the rostrum, where the Christie's auctioneer stands during the auction. Once the auction begins, clients bid against other clients in the room, bid online, or call in to the phone banks that line the edges of the saleroom. At each of the phone banks, impeccably trained Christie's employees relay real-time auction information to their clients and raise their hand with a polite "sir," "ma'am," or "bidding" to signal that their client on the line is bidding. Clients in the room spend their down time quietly flipping through their catalogue and making sure not to wave across the room to a person they know or make any type of sudden movement that might be mistaken for a bid. When their lot comes up on the auction block, they raise their paddle until they are either successful or they are outbid, at which point they give a slight shake of the head or look back down at their catalogue. When Christie's is in high season, there can be as many as eight sales over the course of the week taking place in the morning and then again in the afternoon, day after day, week after week. It is an elegant, lovely way to spend a day.

On the opposite end of the spectrum is benefit auctioneering. Flip through the pages of *Vogue*, *Vanity Fair*, or *Town & Country*, or the party pictures of any magazine, and you will find fabulous pictures of celebrities or socialites attending a gala in New York City that raises money for a nonprofit. Captains of industry, billionaires, and celebrities in black tie and red-carpet-worthy gowns disembark from their chauffeured cars to walk through a barrage of photographers looking for the perfect picture that will be all over the internet only a few minutes later. Seconds after walking in the door, guests are offered a glass of champagne or a specialty cocktail—the first of many drinks over the course of the evening. After roughly an hour of heavy libations, waiters close the bars and encourage begrudging guests to move into an adjoining space for dinner. As guests transition to their tables for the second half of the evening, they are aware that the next couple of hours will be spent listening to honorees give long-winded speeches that they promised would be only two minutes and eating a heavy meal complete with a few glasses of wine. By the time the benefit auctioneer walks onstage toward the end of the evening, it's a miracle if there are five people in the room who have any intention of paying attention to the auction. And that is if they don't see the beginning of the auction as their moment to duck out to relieve the babysitter or get a solid night's sleep. If auctioneers can keep the crowd's attention for long enough to explain the lots, they are lucky.

It didn't take long for me to realize that a gala event for a benefit auction was a stark difference from the focused energy of the Christie's auction room. It seemed like people were bidding only if they had enough time to look up in the middle of a conversation with their dinner partner. Even at the age of twenty-one, I could clearly see that art auctioneering and benefit auctioneering were two entirely different types of auctioneering, and that the elegant arch of an eyebrow that worked so well to increase bidding in the saleroom at Christie's wouldn't have the same results in a crowded room with guests on their third glass of wine.

As my role in special events increased in scope, I began working with the events manager in charge of placing auctioneers with charities. If the event was high profile, a small team from Christie's would accompany the auctioneers to take care of the spotting (identifying people waving their hands to bid), registering bidders (taking down their contact information so the organization could follow up for payment), or serving as a bid clerk (the person standing next to the auctioneer onstage to assist with identifying buyers).

It was in the capacity as a bid clerk that I first saw the crowd through the eyes of an auctioneer. My role was to stand onstage in a crowded, bustling ballroom and help the auctioneer spot bidders he might not see in the chaotic mass of rowdy, overserved people in front of us. Time and time again I found myself wanting to be the auctioneer—not the person standing next to him feeding him jokes and writing down the paddle numbers of the winning bidders. At the time, all the benefit auctioneers whom I accompanied were men, masters at the Christie's rostrum selling Picassos and Monets with regulated increments and engaged guests. Many of them felt completely uncomfortable selling to a group of unruly, chatty, slightly buzzed guests, which was so different from the structured, sober, systematic selling at an art auction. On numerous occasions, I stood backstage waiting with the auctioneers as they paced back and forth nervously, confiding in me their discomfort with this style of auctioneering. With the truth serum that nerves seem to trigger coursing through their veins, a few of the auctioneers would tell me how much they hated taking the benefit auctions. Since I wasn't the one who had to perform during these auctions, it was easy for me to see what worked and what didn't work when trying to engage the audience. My mother used to say that "patience is a virtue," which I always thought was ludicrous when I was a child. Is there anything worse than waiting for something that you really want? But in this case, patience was exactly what I needed because it gave me time to prepare for the moment when I did have the chance to try out.

Over my first few years serving as bid clerk, I would always try to help our more uncomfortable auctioneers gain a little control over the crowd by whispering jokes to them or suggesting new ways to talk about a particular lot to the audience. There was one auctioneer who would constantly ask me to slip him written notes with jokes during the auctions. Unfortunately, with his thick Swiss accent and not-quite-there comedic timing, it never really worked as well as I hoped for him. I watched as my colleagues sold exciting trips to foreign countries and priceless experiences with celebrities in the same careful, measured way that they sold million-dollar pieces of art. I could see the difference between the auctioneers who fed off the boisterous energy of a gala audience and those who couldn't wait to get off the benefit auction stage and return to the podium at Christie's, where guests didn't fire questions at them in the middle of a sale. Both types of auctioneers possessed incredibly impressive skills, but I was drawn to the uncharted chaos of the benefit auction landscape. The lack of structure in a charity auction setting allowed for selling techniques that would be frowned upon in the saleroom at Christie's. Because in the saleroom at Christie's, there is never a moment when the auctioneer realizes that the thousand people in the room had no idea that an auction was taking place when they arrived at the event that evening. On more than one occasion, as I stood next to one of our auctioneers, watching as his face flushed red because he couldn't even hear himself over the noise from the crowd talking over him, I wanted to grab the microphone and try my hand at commanding the audience.

Three years into my career at Christie's, I finally got my chance.

Over the course of a busy gala season when a number of our charity auctioneers had agreed to take the auctions, a few had to cancel at the last minute because of travel issues, illness, or immediate business that took priority over a charity auction. This left more than one of our top clients in a precarious position. Nonprofits rely heavily on the amount raised during their auctions to fill gaps in their operating budgets, fund programs, or even pay salaries. Imagine how it feels when you are counting on the expertise of a trained auctioneer to get every penny out of the crowd, only to be left with someone's uncle who volunteers to fill in at the last minute. As you might imagine, a professional auctioneer has a specific skill set that drives the bidding and delivers impressive results. Someone's uncle? Best-case scenario is he does stand-up comedy on the side and can hold the attention of a crowd. Worst-case, they end up with one-third of their expected budget.

The powers that be at Christie's made an executive decision to open up the annual tryouts to the entire company. Up until that point, the only people who could try out to be charity auctioneers were officers in the company—meaning assistant vice presidents and above. The bulk of the charity auctioneers had been with Christie's for at least ten years by then. Many of them were already tired because of demanding travel schedules and family commitments followed by late nights spent at auctions. In stark contrast, I was a young single woman who had been at the company for three years and had never even had someone suggest that I take a business trip. Add to the fact that I had moved to the city with very few friends and my social calendar wasn't exactly packed. I had nothing but time on my hands, and the prospect of filling that time onstage at black-tie galas across the country seemed like a pretty fabulous opportunity. I didn't fit the typical auctioneer profile by any stretch of the imagination. But it was the moment I had been waiting for, and I went into the saleroom prepared to do anything to pass the tryouts.

I tried out with a class of twenty people—four women and sixteen men. It was a little like the show *Survivor*—every day people were voted off and you came back to a class with fewer people. On the first day, I sat in class with my boss and my boss's boss. After the first round of cuts later that afternoon, I watched as my boss's boss was cut. (She had a voice that disappeared to a whisper when she was nervous.) On the second day, my boss decided to withdraw from tryouts because each time she got up in front of the crowd, she felt positively ill. By the end of the second day, a senior vice president in the company was eliminated along with another ten people. By day three, I started to think that there was a chance I would be in the final round of cuts.

On the final day, the judges sent us back up on the podium and told us to sell anything they threw at us—trips, priceless experiences, even the other students in the class. I did exactly what I had seen so many of the auctioneers do when I accompanied them as a bid clerk. I pretended to be a distinguished British gentleman. In fact, I am pretty sure I was affecting a British accent for much of the class. I acted exactly like everyone I had ever seen take an art auction: calm, measured, formal, polite, giving exact trip details and specifics about the experiences. Whatever I did that day worked. I passed the class with three men. Two of whom were British.

During my "final assessment," the judges explained that I would be a good addition to the team, that it would be nice to have a young woman to send out to the smaller auctions where our top clients weren't front and center, and that I was very "Christie's" in my look, meaning they felt confident that I would show up for auctions dressed appropriately for the event and act professionally while I was there. In a way, I like being underestimated. That way, when I exceed expectations, it feels like a huge accomplishment instead of something that was assumed. I distinctly remember the head of auctioneering telling me that I played "the part of a Christie's auctioneer very well." But one of the judges that year had an acting background and was looking through my performance with a different lens. Her feedback was quite different. "Stop playing auctioneer, Lydia. You look good up there, but I want you to use what you say to us in the moments between each lot to engage the crowd."

I knew what she meant. I specialize in the under-the-breath one-line zinger. Growing up in a four-child family, I needed it to stay afloat with my funny, competitive siblings. I am comfortably sandwiched between two brothers with a whip-smart little sister who rounds us out. Boy, girl, boy, girl. Perfectly symmetrical, incredibly competitive, and a menace on the dance floor. Humor is a big part of my relationship with my siblings—one-upping each other with quick wit is an Olympic sport in our house. Dinner with my siblings is basically one of us throwing another one under the bus in order to make my parents or whatever audience we have laugh. My older brother is usually spared, since he tends to be the kindest, but I show no mercy to my younger siblings and vice versa. The sound of my siblings laughing is one of my favorite things in life, possibly matched only by the sound of my husband and children laughing. But when I passed the auctioneering class, I was in my early twenties. So as I did with most advice I received at that age, I nodded in agreement, assumed I knew better, and disregarded her advice. Frankly, I didn't give that phrase—"playing auctioneer"—another thought for many years.

A couple of weeks after the tryouts, I received my first request for a benefit auction. A winter auction in Kansas City. I couldn't have been more thrilled. My *first business trip*! When you are in your early twenties and spend most days either at your desk or going to meetings around your office, the thought of an all-expenses-paid vacation anywhere sounds great. Winter in Kansas City? Sounded like a dream. Off I went from a freezing New York City to an arctic Kansas City.

I distinctly remember walking into one of the top restaurants in Kansas City to meet the auction committee the day before the auction. The committee was composed of a small group of elderly men and women, and I could see genuine concern on their faces when I walked into the private room armed with a booklet of information about their auction. One of the men kept looking at the door, as if I was the warm-up act and the real auctioneer was going to stroll in any minute. Their surprise at having a female auctioneer was probably surpassed only by the fact that I was the same age as most of their grandchildren. Remember, when I first became an auctioneer, people didn't Google you before you walked in the door. Your reputation was everything, and since this was my first auction, I didn't have a reputation. There were definitely jokes made about moving me from the head table to the kids' table. Nevertheless, I had spent a few full days getting ready for the auction and their fear seemed to lessen when it was clear

I had come prepared. Of course I was prepared: this was it—the moment I had been waiting for.

After a long day spent indoors at the hotel readying myself for the auction, I arrived at the museum where the auction was taking place feeling like a ball of nerves. I remember standing backstage with the event organizer revising my notes and feeling positively ill from stage fright.

"Ladies and gentleman, please welcome Lydia Fenet from Christie's Auction House." I felt like I was moving through water as I slowly walked onto the stage, nervously looking at the crowd of a few hundred guests who were paying absolutely no attention to me. I stood in front of the small podium clutching the gavel I had borrowed from the bids department at Christie's like my life depended on it. I put my notes down on the podium, spread them out, and cleared my throat. "Good evening, ladies and gentlemen." A few people glanced up, but the majority of the crowd continued talking. I stood there for a second and then banged down my gavel a few times. A few more people turned around and looked up.

Well, that seemed to work a little better.

I did it again. Louder this time.

Whenever I return to my table after an auction, people always want to see the gavel. You know, the thing that Judge Judy keeps directly in front of her while she is watching two people duke it out over a cable box payment. That she slams down forcefully as she makes the final verdict. What you don't realize until you use a gavel is that they aren't meant to be hammered down repeatedly. They are meant to be slammed down once, maybe twice, loud enough to make an impactful sound but not hard enough to break the top of the gavel off the handle. Which is what happened to me. That's right, the force of the blow to the gavel broke the handle from the smaller hammer part, and I watched it roll in slow motion under the podium. Words like "mortifying," "embarrassing," and "swallow me up please, stage," come to my mind. I didn't really know what to do, so I kneeled down in my cocktail dress and fished the broken head of the gavel out from under the podium.

Right. Let's try that again. I hit the top of the gavel down and started the auction.

Now this is the part of the story when I wish I could tell you that I rocked the auction like it had never been rocked before. That I raised five times what they wanted and had the crowd eating out of my hand. Truth be told, the auction was fine. Just fine. I raised the money the committee needed, but from where I stood onstage, the entire thing felt flat. The audience talked the entire time despite my efforts to quiet them, and it felt like I was taking an auction to a crowd of distant observers. After I said good night to the committee, I returned to my hotel room feeling tired and deflated. I'd had such high expectations for what I was going to be able to do onstage but, in fact, I defaulted to exactly what I had seen everyone else do.

The next few years passed in much the same fashion. I was considered a good, solid auctioneer, and as a result I was asked back to the organizations that had used me previously. Whereas I had started off taking twenty auctions my first year, in the years that followed that number quickly escalated to thirty, fifty, then seventy auctions a year. I was still taking auctions the way I took them when I'd tried out, the same way that I had seen those before me do it time and time again. I remember those first years onstage as busy and fun—certainly more exciting than sitting in my apartment in New York City missing my friends from college and eating takeout by myself. But for the most part, the auctions always seemed to be the same—slightly painful. I would get onstage after dessert was served, take far too many auction lots, which I assumed I had to do since the other auctioneers did it, and watch as people began to file out of the event to get home. Those who remained would smile politely and listen in an almost pitying way. Eventually they would tire of listening to me call numbers out in an increasingly loud voice to drown out their chatter, at which point they would turn back to their tablemates and start talking again.

But the crowd's lack of interest in the auction had nothing to do with my volume level. What I was saying wasn't grabbing their attention—I was just repeating numbers in a sequence. In a way, I almost sympathized with them. I would prefer a glass of wine and a chat with a friend over listening to someone spouting numbers for something that I have no intention of buying any day of the week. For many of our charity auctioneers, this is the point when they simply stop taking auctions. Being onstage night after night while people ignore you does not do much for one's self-confidence. After another painful season, auctioneers eventually reduce the number of auctions they'll take to the point that they start to fear the ones they do take once or twice a year—and then they stop taking them completely.

I hadn't hit that point yet, but I was starting to lose enthusiasm for what I had once thought was going to be something I was born to do. Nevertheless, I kept signing up for the auctions whenever I could, as it still gave me something to do in the evenings. I needed to prove to myself that I could do better. I just didn't know what better was yet. *Yet.*

Five years into my auctioneering career, I woke up one Saturday morning feeling absolutely horrible. A nasty flu had been going around and it had finally caught up with me. Normally this would have been an excuse to lie in bed all day with a good book and a bottle of Gatorade, but I was scheduled to take an auction that evening. I remember lying under the covers shivering as I scrolled down the numbers of other auctioneers on my flip phone. Between naps I called the auctioneers one by one, growing increasingly desperate as each declined to fill in for me for a different reason. By the time I heard the final no, it was clear that I was going to have to take the auction no matter how horrendous I was feeling. I stayed in bed flat on my back the entire day until an hour before the auction, when I took a double dose of DayQuil, put on my most comfortable black dress and the lowest pair of heels I could find, and basically crawled to the Boathouse, a stunning venue overlooking a lake in Central Park, to take the auction. On any other night I would have been thrilled to be spending time in this gorgeous setting, surrounded by the glittering views of New York City. Instead I sat huddled in a chair in the corner of the room nursing a ginger ale and feeling like I was going to pass out. As they wrangled the crowd into the room for dinner after the cocktail hour, I slowly moved my chair right beside the stage until they announced my name.

What I didn't know at that point was the adrenaline that begins to course through your body in the moments right before you go onstage makes you feel much better. So as the Voice of God announced my name to start the live auction, I started to feel a little bit like me. But a little bit like me was not enough to transform me into my usual British-gentleman auctioneering persona. In that moment I felt so awful that I couldn't pretend to be anyone—anyone but me. And so I stopped "playing" auctioneer and started selling the lots the way that I would sell them to my friends.

The first lot up for sale was a private tour of an art collection at the home of a board member. Years before, I had been sitting next to this woman at a Christie's lunch the day after I'd been dumped by a guy out of left field. Like heartbroken, never-getting-over-it, thought-I-was-going-to-die broken-up-with out of left field. After sitting down for the lunch, instead of talking to her about the fabulous art that was coming up in the next sale, I spent the entire lunch with tears rolling down my cheeks, trying to keep it together while I felt like my entire world was crumbling. So professional, right? She listened kindly, gave great advice about things to do post-breakup (wine, chocolate, repeat), and handed me her napkin when my tears had soaked through the one on my lap. So instead of reading off the lot the way that I would have normally described it—private tour of a beautiful apartment, amazing art collection, cocktails, the whole nine yards—I told the audience that the hostess obviously had an amazing art collection, lived in a beautiful apartment, and would serve delicious cocktails, but more importantly, she was the next Oprah. If you needed relationship advice, needed a good cry or advice about what to do when someone dumped you, this would be your opportunity to spend some quality time with her. *Take it from me—I would know.*

This very small change in selling—inserting something from my own life into that moment—made people stop talking and listen. In that moment it clicked. A lightbulb went off. Sell as myself. Sell as me. Why would I bore someone with the details of a lot without creating a story for the person in front of me? I am a storyteller in every sense of the word. When I try to make a point, it comes in the form of a story. Life. Story. Everything seems better with a setup at the beginning, an interesting middle, and a grand finale with a little flair.

That was what I was missing. My auction lots needed a story.

First lot: *sold* for three times the estimate. *That* is what I had been waiting for.

"Lot number two, ladies and gentlemen . . ." The second lot up for sale was a vacation at a home in Mexico with a large number of bedrooms and bathrooms, an infinity pool, and a private chef. Instead of listing the specifics of the house, I led with a quick one-liner about my college trip to Mexico and how lucky the winning bidder was that they would not end their trip on a slide at Señor Frog's. As I described the Mexico lot with a few more jokes thrown in, I noticed that people had physically turned their chairs to face the stage. Now *that* was a good sign. I pressed on cautiously, inserting a few more jokes, mentioning a couple of dresses that I liked on women who were bidding, drawing parallels between people in the audience and their celebrity doppelgängers, making up names for people who were too shy to give me their names—all of these things were woven into the fabric of the auction. It was only when I started talking *to* the audience instead of *at* the audience, and incorporating things that I was noticing in the room into the auction, that the crowd started to engage. And the more I realized that people had stopped talking over me and were actually listening to what I was saying, the more I came alive; and the more I came alive, the more fun they had.

The auction was no longer about numbers and boring trip details; it was about the fantasy of a vacation to the turquoise water of the Caribbean in the dead of winter. Priceless experiences with celebrities were no longer about just the experience itself, but also the hope that you would run into your high school frenemy while

LYDIA FENET

hanging out on your lunch date with George Clooney or (when Instagram arrived on the scene) that you could turn your followers from 50 to 55 million with a picture from your dinner out with Brad Pitt. Well, maybe not 55 million, but at least 100. I turned the focus from what I was selling to the person I was selling it to, and the audience was in on every level. The auction was no longer just an auction; it was a story where the audience members were part of the story line. Everyone likes to be noticed, whether they are bidding or not. Most people enjoy being recognized even if it is a quick compliment for raising their hand to bid. Once everyone realized they could potentially be included in this play, they were suddenly rapt with attention. When the auction was over, despite the chills and fever that reappeared only minutes after I'd left the stage to fall into the back seat of a cab, I felt elated. *This* was what I had been missing all these years. Selling as me.

With another twenty-five auctions left that season, I had plenty of time to practice my new style. Goodbye formal auctioneer persona, fake British accent, and formal stance behind the podium. What I had seen that night at the Boathouse was not an aberration. The crowd responded differently when I was onstage selling as myself, and I felt engaged and excited by the difference in the crowd. Auctions were no longer about getting out of my apartment so that I wasn't sitting by myself eating takeout. The stage had become a place that I couldn't wait to get back to as many times as possible to practice this newfound skill. As I took more and more auctions, I realized that using a little of that southern charm I had watched my grandmother and my mother use could win people over even when the situation seemed unwinnable, and a lot of humor could dramatically increase the bidding and also keep the audience engaged. It turns out that making people laugh also makes them want to

36

spend money. Laughter brings people together, engages them, and makes what had previously felt like a chore feel fun and fresh. Most importantly, it also keeps them quiet! I am usually onstage before a crowd of five hundred to five thousand people, so whatever I am saying has to interest them enough to keep them from talking to the other people at their table—and I prefer humor over shock value any day of the week.

Obviously, the result of this could have been just that I was having more fun onstage and the audience was paying attention, but the real result was, as it often is, in the numbers. I was raising 20, 30, 40, even 50 percent more than organizations had previously raised during their auctions. I was returning to auctions I had taken in past years and blowing my sales results out of the water. As word of my different approach to selling started to spread in the nonprofit world, I began receiving more and more requests. Our top clients were emailing to ask senior executives if I could take their auctions. Not only did they notice, but they started recommending me to their top clients as well.

The way that I command the stage now is completely different from the way I did when I started auctioneering almost fifteen years ago. My auctioneering persona now is sales through the prism of my life. My selling approach has evolved as my life has evolved. When I took that auction at the Boathouse in my twenties, I was taking an auction as a single woman who had been dumped by a boyfriend. Was there anyone in that audience—male or female—who didn't relate on some level? Relating, sharing, offering a ten-second glimpse into my life made the audience feel like I was in it with them. As I returned year after year to organizations to take their auctions, I would offer myself as an additional guest in case the person bidding didn't have enough friends to fill a party of fifty people. When my sister or brother accompanied me as a guest for an auction, I would throw them into the package after inquiring whether or not the person bidding was single. I even had friends *request* to accompany me to auctions on the off chance I would offer them in a package. When auctioning off trips to places I had been, I threw in a quick story or comment about the place—eat here, drink here, *do not do this*. When I took auctions while nine months pregnant with each of my three kids, my selling technique was to lean on the sympathy of any women in the audience to raise money quickly so I could get offstage and put my feet up. When I started taking auctions again four weeks after having my third baby, you had better believe I told the audience that it was their responsibility to get me home as quickly as possible to nurse the baby. When I get onstage, I want everyone attending the auction to have a blast, whether it be the waiters serving the guests, the guests attending the event, or the biggest bidder in the room. The woman who works at the coat check at Cipriani Wall Street took my coat last year as I walked in for an auction, gave me a thumbs-up, and said, "It's auction time." Better believe it. Get me on that stage!

Now, I realize that 99 percent of the women reading this book are not going to be selling auction lots from a stage. Or maybe you are, in which case I hope you absolutely crush it. But for the rest of you who don't feel like you are getting the results that you want from your life, your job, or even an interview, think about the way that you are communicating yourself to other people. What I have learned selling both from onstage and also in my full-time job at Christie's running a global department called strategic partnerships is that people respond when you are selling as yourself. Selling is as much about relationships as it is about business, so the more natural you feel while you are selling something, the more likely someone is to believe that what you are saying is true. When I sell something, it is rare that you will hear me do it without framing it within the context of a story or inserting a one-liner here and there, which, as you now know, is a great way to engage an audience. It puts me at ease to be able to sell something in a way that seems natural—and people respond when you are acting in an authentic way.

When I tell you to "sell as yourself," I want you to think about how you can use this advice in everyday life. Watch how people respond when you are selling or presenting. Are their eyes glazing over as you talk? Are they looking at their phone? Are they nodding but when you stop talking do they try to leave without so much as a goodbye? Next, consider how you are selling. The exact way that you were taught to sell? Hard driving and relentless when you would prefer to get to know the person in front of you so that you understand their objectives? Dead serious when your quick wit is what your friends would say is your best quality? Are you putting on a completely different persona like I was for my first five years onstage? Remember that you have to believe in yourself and in what you are selling in order for other people to believe in it too. It takes energy to pretend to be someone else, and I prefer to use that energy to nail the sale.

The Most Powerful Woman in the Room is authentic in the way that she sells herself and her vision to other people. She is unafraid of presenting who she is and what she has accomplished. She believes that hard work and practice will ultimately help her obtain everything she wants in life. She knows that people will believe in her when she believes in what she is selling and when she uses her best quality—her personality—to bring people along on her journey.

how they sell as themselves

MIA KANG

Model and Activist

From the age of thirteen, I tortured myself through every eating and body-dysmorphic disorder you can imagine because I thought I had to look a certain way, dictated by the fashion industry and society. I have been able to let go of these standards, but as someone who has largely contributed to this machine, I feel a responsibility and duty to do what is in my power to correct it so that the next generation of girls does not have to go through what I went through.

I strive to show the industry that the healthy, strong, educated, opinionated, and secure woman standing before them today is the type of woman that we need on our billboards and in our magazines, not the insecure, unhealthy girl who fits into all the sample sizes. That girl is long gone. We have enough models—women are in dire need of some role models.

When I came back from learning Muay Thai or Thai boxing—more fit than ever but also larger than those sample sizes—I needed to sell my new self to a world that was not used to seeing this body. So this is how I marketed myself to the first person I needed to, my agent.

"Listen, this is who I am. I'm healthy now. I'm happy now. I have a story to tell. I see a problem, and I think that we all see that problem.

We need to show women how to be healthy, confident, to stop letting our insecurities weigh us down, and that what matters is the woman that you are and not what size clothes you wear. And I want to be that person to show them."

I held my breath as I waited for her reply.

She said, "Let's do this."

MARTHA STEWART

Emmy Award–winning television show host, entrepreneur, bestselling author, and America's most trusted lifestyle expert

I have always considered myself a teacher, and I firmly believe that in order to teach, you have to truly dedicate yourself to learning what it is you are teaching. The same can be said for selling and selling yourself. You have to know your subject matter through and through. Be confident in who you are and persevere. Have enough confidence to keep pressing forward whether or not people seem to like you. Look for opportunities around you and start with your own expertise. Defend your ideas, but be flexible. Success seldom comes in exactly the form you imagine it will.

THE MOST
POWERFUL
WOMAN
IN THE
ROOM . . .

3

knows you are
what you negotiate

I f I had a dollar for every time I told someone that I loved my job when I was in my twenties, my Instagram feed would contain pictures of private jets instead of Delta Comfort+ seats. And while I was very good at my job, I didn't spend much time thinking about my company as a larger organization—or how I might need to advocate for myself internally. I thought that if I kept my head down, did my job well, and was a good colleague internally and externally, someone would surely notice and promote me. What I didn't realize is that just because you are good at your job doesn't mean that you will be adequately compensated for your ability.

In my twenties, I lived and breathed work. I worked ten- to fourteen-hour days, six to seven days a week, eleven and a half months out of the year. But in New York, working nonstop is part of the culture, and it didn't seem unusual that by the end of my first year, our small team had already churned out more than five hundred events. Because of the relentless pace of my job, I had plenty of time to learn it inside and out. Aside from long runs that I would take along the Hudson River Park running path whenever I had a spare moment, I rarely left the office. I spent my first five years working closely with everyone on the events team as the coordinator of the department when, over the course of six months, both the manager and the director of the department left to pursue other jobs. Never one to pass up an opportunity, I immediately lobbied for the position of director of the department. Although there were a number of conversations about whether they should interview externally, ultimately they felt that I was the only one who had enough experience to fill the role, and so at the age of twenty-six, I was promoted to head of special events for Christie's Americas.

Client entertaining is hugely important in the auction business, as our clients are among the wealthiest individuals in the world. The level of expectation for each and every event is incredibly high, since you entertain billionaires, celebrities, and world leaders together in one room many times over the course of a year. Because I was promoted to head of the department at such a young age, I wanted to ensure that people took me seriously and, to me, that meant being the first in the door and the last out the door. My parents always drilled the importance of a strong work ethic into me, along with the belief that I could do anything or be anyone I wanted to be as long as I applied myself. I prided myself on being in my office promptly at 8:30 a.m. in case our chairman called (as he liked to do at 8:30 a.m.) to ask questions about who was attending the events that day or what we had chosen to serve at those events. In the evening, I would stay until our last guest left a reception or dinner to ensure that we were delivering a seamless experience before heading home or out to meet my friends. I spent so much time at the office that my personal life was completely interwoven into the fabric of my job. As a result, I came to think of my job and the company where I worked as my extended family.

I loved my job so much that I wholeheartedly believed my boss, whom I adored, when he told me how excited I should be to work for the "glamour of the job." Anytime I got up the courage to ask for a raise, he would kindly remind me how lucky I was to be working for Christie's, the world's leading auction business, and how many other women around the world would kill for my job. Not only did I believe him, but I perpetuated this myth by telling my team the same thing. It never occurred to me that I should challenge that thinking or that the skill set that I had grown over many late nights was worth additional compensation. I was lucky! I should be thankful for the opportunity to work at Christie's. So when I was promoted to head of events, I didn't think to challenge the minuscule pay increase I received. I had received a big title, and, of course, I was working for the glamour of the job.

So listen carefully when I say this, because I want you to be absolutely sure that you understand: No matter how much you love your job, your company, your role, you are going to be compensated adequately only by negotiating for what you deserve. You can be the smartest and strongest in your field, but you are the only one who is going to fight for the compensation that you ultimately receive. What I wish for each and every one of you is that you find something that makes you excited to get out of bed today—whether it be a place of work, a company that you have built, or simply an idea that you have to make something happen. But take it from me, someone in your company is making money from doing their job, and if you are excelling at work, it might as well be you. Being gainfully employed is a blessing—finding a job can be challenging—but if you are consistently getting strong performance reviews, receiving praise, or even just feel that you are exceeding the parameters of your original job description, research what other people in that position are making so that you don't take a dime less than you deserve. I don't mean if you arrived at work two weeks ago and think that you deserve a raise; I mean that you have put in the time, learned your job, and then started to work at a much higher level than you were originally hired. If you are in doubt, ask your friends or even colleagues for honest advice about whether or not you are in a place where you deserve a promotion. Don't ask someone who always says yes—you are looking for someone to give you honest feedback.

I learned this lesson the hard way about ten years into my career at Christie's. By that point, most of my friends were a decade into their careers. Many had either moved into fairly prominent roles or had moved from company to company to receive larger titles with bigger compensation packages. I speak on behalf of most of my squad; those years were fun and fantastic. We were young(ish), and most of us were unmarried and therefore could easily attend one another's work parties, collaborate together, travel together, and work insanely long hours in order to stay on top of our game. After ten years in special events, four years as the head of the department, I could do my job with my eyes closed and one hand behind my back while FaceTiming from a different country. I was trusted by the senior executives in my company and had built a strong team who consistently delivered excellent results despite the demanding, intense schedule.

One Sunday over brunch, I told my friends that my roommate had lost her job and was moving out of the apartment. I needed a roommate in the next month and asked them to reach out to anyone who might be looking to make a move. Everyone volunteered an idea or two, but one of my friends was quiet throughout the entire conversation. Toward the end of the meal, she announced to the group that she had some exciting news: she was buying a one-bedroom apartment on her own. While outwardly I expressed my excitement for this move, and even offered to bring over a bottle of wine to celebrate after she moved in, I was floored. I thought we were all in the same boat, living on a relatively paltry salary but compensated by the experiences and excitement provided by our jobs. Who needs to buy food when you can eat at the cocktail parties at work? I was living in a one-bedroom apartment where my roommate and I had built a wall to divide the living room in half to make a second bedroom. Sure it was a doorman, elevator building, but there was no way that I would be buying a one bedroom. EVER. Well over half of my salary was going to rent. I could barely speak. I felt sick. But truthfully, I had no one to blame but myself; I was getting exactly what I had negotiated. I was hurt and embarrassed, but more than anything, it finally motivated me to question if I was getting adequately compensated for my job.

Even though I was motivated, at the time I didn't even know where to start. Today you can pull up websites with plenty of information for salary comparisons, but ten years ago there wasn't a handy resource like that on my radar. I started by doing market research the way I knew how—by asking my peers about their compensation as well as asking for intel about any friends they had in relevant industries. It felt unnatural at first; I had always been told that talking about money was tacky, but for once I really didn't care. It didn't take me long to realize I was making less than half of what most people in a similar position made in my field. The part that really killed me, however, was that during this particular time, a new head of human resources had transitioned into the role. We had become friendly as I trained him to be a charity auctioneer. One afternoon he pulled me aside and said, "You know, we should really talk about your comp. You are actually making way below market value."

I went home, sat on my bed, and wept. I couldn't understand where I had gone wrong. I worked as hard as I could, dedicated myself to my job, and did everything I was supposed to do. Why hadn't someone noticed?

I'll tell you why.

Because I didn't ask.

For anything.

I accepted everything that was given to me with a polite "thank you so much" and went on without giving it a second thought. Why would I think or talk about money with anyone? It was one of those topics that, growing up in a polite family, I thought I shouldn't discuss. A topic that I shouldn't bring up in conversation with my peers. Why? Because it's rude. It's insensitive. It makes people uncomfortable. And if you don't really understand why you need money or what it does or why knowing about it is so important, then you should just ignore it and let someone else deal with it.

Now hit Select All and erase that entire paragraph from your brain for the rest of your life.

Educating yourself about money—how to use it, how to spend it, how to make it, how to save it, how to make more of it—is one of the most important things you can do in your life. It doesn't matter if you are the CEO of your family or the CEO at an office or the CEO of a bunch of great ideas. Do not think simply because you are a woman or because you are married to someone who is good at taking care of money or because your parents still take care of you or because you delete emails alerting you about your rising credit card minimum payments that you aren't responsible for understanding where your money comes from or where it goes. You and only you are responsible for your financial security: for educating yourself and understanding what it means to be in good financial standing. If you are someone who is in good shape financially and are nodding while you are reading this paragraph, take a look around you and reach out to friends you think could benefit from a "Money 101" conversation. Opening the dialogue with friends who don't understand the importance of financial wellness is an incredible gift, as a lot of them might be afraid to ask because they feel like they should already know the answer. Helping a friend understand the importance of money in life is one of the greatest gifts you can give someone. Money is power, yes. But knowledge about money is even more powerful in life and in business.

I had a crash course in learning about the importance of money three years earlier as head of special events. As I was in the middle of setting up for a fabulous party we were holding to kick off New York Fashion Week alongside our upcoming contemporary art sale, my boss pulled me into his office and told me that Lehman Brothers was about to collapse. At the time I didn't know what it meant, but from the look on his face I could tell it wasn't good. Seemingly overnight, the financial world came to a crashing halt. As happened with most companies at that time, I was told that I was going to need to fire a member of my team because we were going to immediately cut back on events given the current economic climate. The problem was that, after having been through many rounds of layoffs at that point, I knew I would never get that head count back after the market eventually picked up again. Which meant that we would still be producing hundreds of events with two members of staff. I also knew that despite the downturn in the market, there was no way we were going to halt having events completely. We would continue having sales, which meant we would continue having events. I proposed an idea to my boss: I had been getting a lot of other companies to give us money in exchange for letting them put their branding on our invitations, invite a few of their clients to our events, and also meet our clients at the events. I told my boss that if I could just keep my team intact, in 2009 I would not use the events budget we had been allocated, but rather I would get other companies to sponsor every event that we had. He gave me six months to prove I could do it.

I empowered my team to be the architects of their own success. To keep their jobs, they needed to look at each event as a puzzle and try to find the different pieces that would complete it. We needed every element of the event—invitations, food, alcohol, rentals—underwritten. These were tough times for our traditional sponsors (banks, fashion houses, and car companies), but there are always smaller companies looking to get their name out in front of the right clients, especially if they have tiny marketing budgets. We called hot new restaurants and asked them to contribute food and staffing at no cost to us in exchange for getting branding on invitations that we sent out to our top clients around the city. We called PR companies to find out about new liquor companies that were launching and offered to include their products in our events with prominent placement in our central staircase. We cold-called fledgling letterpress companies and gave them the opportunity to get their products into the hands of their target clients by producing invitations for our events. Six months in, we hadn't spent a penny of our budget, and at the end of the year we had made a profit. For the next two years I continued to run the department in the same way, despite the gradual reversal in the financial market, and it continued to work. We continued to make money, and then more money. As crazy as it sounds, I never thought that I should be the person who received any type of bonus or compensation for making this happen. I worked for the glory of the brand, the glamour of the job, remember? But until that moment at brunch with my friends, it had never occurred to me that I should be making the kind of money that would allow me to buy an apartment. Nor that I should be compensated for having turned a department that had traditionally been an expense into a revenue-generating department. I was just happy to keep my team in place and get a "well done" from senior management.

And because I don't want you to make the same mistake along the way, I want to lay out three things that I wish someone had told me earlier in my career so that I could have been the one announcing over brunch that I was buying a one-bedroom apart-ment instead of sobbing on my bed that day. Remember these things as you think about how you are going to be compensated appropriately for your work.

1. *Your company is a business.* At the end of the day, the success of a company is based on more money coming in than money going out. Companies want more money coming in than they want going out, so ultimately they will want to pay you the least amount that you will accept and still agree to come to work each day. I don't want to use the phrase "your company is just not that into you," but when it comes to paying you, your company is only going to be as into you as much as it needs to be in order to keep you for a second date.

2. *Lose the emotion.* If you are good at your job, you should be compensated for your work. If you love to cry as much as I do, watch something that makes you cry the day or even the night before you go into any negotiation. Don't get me wrong. I have a great respect for crying—I think it is a fantastic human emotion. But it has no place in the office. You need to get your tears out so that you are ready to negotiate like a boss.

3. *Don't apologize.* So many women on my teams over the years have come into my office around performance review time and started with, "I'm sorry to ask this but . . ." You shouldn't be sorry. If you deserve a raise, I am happy to fight on your behalf. I just need to know what you want when I am going in to speak to human resources. In some cases I may not be able to get you what you want, but I can certainly try. And if I don't think that you are ready for that promotion or I don't feel that you are at a point in your career where you should be receiving additional compensation, I will tell you that too. Even if someone doesn't give you what you want at that exact moment, you are still setting up an expectation for what you will want in the future, so you are giving them something to aim toward as you move up in your career. But also be ready to hear news that you may not like but need to hear in order to get more compensation. You may not be doing as well as you think you are doing. And hearing that does not feel great, but you need to understand what it is going to take for you to get to the place that you want. The truth can be hard to hear, but hearing the good, bad, or ugly can help you adjust your actions to achieve a raise.

I pride myself on the ability to never take a short view of a long game, even when a deal goes south or I don't like the outcome of a situation. I try not to jump to conclusions and make impulsive decisions. Instead I prefer to sit back, take time to create a plan, and then methodically plot out every step of that plan so that I anticipate any curveballs that might come my way. And then I execute it.

After some serious soul searching, I came to the conclusion that, ten years into a career that I loved, at a company I loved working for, I didn't want to leave. Instead I wanted to be compensated for the job that I was already doing and reach even higher; I wanted to create a new department for the company.

But first I needed to do some research. And then I needed to come up with a plan. After the conversations that I'd had with my peers and the new head of human resources, I decided it was time to see what my value was on the open market. I heard about a head of communications job at one of the world's top luxury brands that required an in-depth knowledge of event production. After scouring the job description, I felt confident that I had what they needed for the job. I submitted my résumé and was promptly called by the head of human resources to come in for an interview. I went to meet with her armed with mounds of research about the company as well as a list of questions about the job, the company, and the expectations for the person in the role. The meeting went well, and at the end of our allotted time, she asked if I could meet with the CEO, who was leaving the following week for an extended trip. Thus I found myself sitting outside his office as he finished up a meeting with Justin Timberlake. Yes, JT. Yes, I was dying.

After Justin had exited the office (and I nearly passed out), the CEO's assistant called me into his office and we started discussing the position. He was honest about the hours, the travel, and the intense nature of the job, but more importantly, he was honest about the compensation. Which was almost four times as much as I was making in my job.

And that, my friends, was all it took to light the fire under me.

At first I was angry at everyone else—my company, my boss, anyone who had ever seen my quality of work and not advocated for me. But truthfully, I was just angry at myself for not being confident enough to expect that I was worth more and follow through to make sure that I was getting it. In addition, I was annoyed with myself for never asking around—of being too proud to talk to my friends about salary and compensation. Had I started having those conversations with my friends years ago, I would have realized that I was seriously underpaid and perhaps could have started initiating these salary negotiations at an earlier age. Take it from someone who has worked in New York for twenty years, you are only going to get what you negotiate for yourself. If you want something, you have to show passion and dedication to constantly innovating and improving yourself—and you are going to have to work for it. I can find people who will advocate for and mentor me, but I have to road-map what I want so that they can help me on my journey.

Although I was still enjoying my position as head of events, I was also tiring of the frenetic pace of a high-stress events job combined with a high-stress night job as a charity auctioneer. I was ready for a change. I figured if I was going to push for the pay raise that I deserved, I should also make the career transition that I was looking to make at the same time. I needed to use the momentum I had created by pushing my team into action while most people around me were still bemoaning the fact that the stock market had plummeted overnight and the financial world had been turned upside down. I wrote a business plan for a new department called "strategic partnerships" that would create large-scale global partnerships for Christie's based on the model I had used in 2008—but instead of making a small profit, I projected that we could make a couple of million in revenue, ostensibly turning what had been a support department into a profit center. Christie's has an untarnished brand, and I wanted to capitalize on that brand to make money for the company.

Once the seeds of this idea began to grow into actionable plans, I looked at the landscape in front of me to figure out the best way to move this forward. One thing that I saw as a potential road-block: my boss, whom I adored, truly believed that we worked for the glory of saying that we worked for Christie's. I knew that he wasn't fighting for a raise for himself, so I knew that it would be difficult for him to justify fighting for the kind of pay raise I was looking for on my new path. I needed someone else to look at my plan and tell me if he thought it could work on a larger scale. Our chief marketing officer had recently joined the company. Judging by the size of his office and his impressive résumé, I was certain that he wasn't working for the glory of any brand but his own. I waited until he was in town from London later that month and scheduled fifteen minutes on his calendar to explain my idea. I prepared for this meeting in much the same way that I suggest you prepare for any type of interview or meeting—über prepared, having tried to anticipate any questions and being ready with a short list of action points so that he felt invested in my idea. Much to my excitement, he agreed that the idea could work and offered practical advice on how to move things forward internally. But I didn't report to our chief marketing officer, so the next step was figuring out how to get a promotion and a pay raise from my current boss.

When my boss returned from London, I asked another colleague with whom he was good friends to casually mention that he heard I was interviewing for another job. I didn't have a written offer from the other company, but I felt confident that it was coming. It just wasn't coming soon enough. We were two weeks away from the big November sales and I had three new team members who had just started on the events team one year prior. There was no one on the events team at that time who had the contacts, relationships, and Rolodex to execute the upcoming events. In short, I held the power. And more importantly, I knew I held the power, so I walked into the negotiation without fear.

My husband, whom I was dating at the time, asked me on more than one occasion as I set my plan into motion, "Aren't you nervous? What if they don't offer you anything? What are you going to do?" Truth be told, I would have stayed anyway until I found a new job that gave me what I was looking for. But I had too much invested by that point to turn around and walk away.

One thing that I can tell you from almost two decades as an auctioneer and as a mom of three small children: people always want something more when someone else has it. And I needed him to believe that I was ready to walk.

It was time to start working for the glory of the most important brand of all.

Mine.

By the time my boss called me into his office, the following pieces were in place:

1. He knew that I was interviewing at another company.
2. Our chief marketing officer confirmed that my business plan was solid and he would support a new department called "strategic partnerships."
3. I knew what other luxury companies were paying for the same job.
4. Christie's was two weeks away from the peak of our busy season—and at that time I was the only one who could execute the number of high-level events to the satisfaction of our CEO.

The conversation went like this:

My boss: "I have heard from a reliable source that you have been interviewing at another company."

Me, owning it like a boss: "Yes, I have been offered a job at another company. They need me to start in two weeks."

Truthfully, when I walked into his office that morning I hadn't planned to bluff a job offer with a fictional start date, but sitting across from him I knew that I would never have an opportunity like this again.

As we say in my family, "Go big or go home."

His face went sheet white and then red and then a deeper red. He sat there staring at me and then he asked me the question that I had been waiting to hear.

"What will it take to make you stay?"

I had dreamed about this moment, prepared for this moment, and so I launched into my list of demands:

"I want to start a new department called 'strategic partnerships' with a global team to support it. I want a salary commensurate with the new job and the title of global head of strategic partnerships, senior vice president."

I spent the next fifteen minutes outlining my vision for the department, and by the end of my presentation, he simply said, "I'll give human resources a call and get back to you by end of day to let you know exactly what we will give you to stay."

I shook his hand (because when you are owning it, you keep the conversation as formal as possible), walked out of his office, past the door to my office, out the front door of Christie's, and kept walking until the tears began to fall down my face. Tears of joy.

True to his word, he called me later that day and we sat down with the head of human resources, whereby they told me their offer:

1. They agreed with the idea behind strategic partnerships and would allow me to start the department.
2. While they couldn't exactly match the salary of the other "job offer," they could get very close (thereby tripling my salary).
3. They were willing to give me the title of head of the department but would only make me global head of the department once I had signed my first international partnership.

The head of HR slid a piece of paper across the table with all the numbers and their offer and said, "So, step one is that you get everything you want, and then step two, the international title, comes when you sign the first international deal."

There were so many emotions at that moment. I had done the math before I went up to his office. I knew that if I were to get the salary increase that I had asked for, I wouldn't have to find another roommate for my apartment. I would be able to afford a one-bedroom apartment on my own. There was also the other part of the equation—I didn't have a job offer lined up, but I knew that I would never forgive myself if I didn't go all in.

I smiled politely and shook my head and said, "No, you see, because without step one and an international title, there is no step two."

My boss let out a warbled "ugh," and the head of human resources said, "I will be right back."

An hour later he called and said, "New job, new title, new salary—you can come up and sign your new contract later today."

Shortly after I signed the new contract, I called the leasing agent at my building and told her that I would be taking over the new lease on my own. It was an indescribable feeling. I had negotiated what I deserved and had set in motion what I needed to get what I wanted.

In hindsight, waiting to have a job offer in hand probably would have been the safer approach, and one I would certainly recommend if you aren't sure that there will be some type of offer on the table. The Most Powerful Woman in the Room is strong and confident, but she also needs to pay her bills. But sometimes in life you just have to go for it and believe that you are worth what you are asking for.

Years later, after both my boss and the head of HR had left Christie's to pursue other careers, I met up with my old boss for our semiannual dinner. After a couple of glasses of wine I felt like it was time to come clean about the missing job offer. He let out a loud laugh and told me he had always been impressed by the way I held my ground that day. He also told me that he knew I was serious because it was the first time I didn't cry when I was asking for something.

I think back to that day a lot. What if I had never started that conversation, what if I hadn't held my ground, what if I were still doing my old job day after day, hoping that someone would notice?

Chances are I would be doing exactly the same thing. Keeping my head down, doing my job, and splitting a one-bedroom apartment with my best friend.

The Most Powerful Woman in the Room that day was me. I was confident in myself, approached the conversation without tears, without fear, and held my ground.

So remember my story the next time you see something that you want but are afraid to put yourself forward. You are only going to get what you negotiate in life, and no one can advocate for you better than you. The next time you see someone you admire get a promotion or succeed in an area of interest to you, ask for a few minutes of their time and get insight into what it took for them to get what they wanted. Sometimes you have to fake it till you make it—and learning lessons from those who have paved the road in front of you can give you the boost that you need to walk into a conversation or a meeting with a little extra confidence. And if you are a particularly shrewd negotiator, offer advice to people who are floundering in their career. Sometimes an encouraging word from a senior colleague or someone you admire is all it takes. It's time to challenge your own thinking when it comes to what you deserve in life and in business.

Remember, no tears, no fear. Now get out there and negotiate!

THREE OTHER POWERFUL WOMEN ON . . .

their negotiation strategy

GEMMA BURGESS

Author and Screenwriter

When I was living in London in my twenties, permanently broke and in a state of crisis about my professional, financial, and (let's be honest) romantic future, I would tackle any seemingly self-assured woman over thirty-five and beg her to meet me. I would say, "I'll buy you coffee anywhere you like, if you tell me your life story and give me advice." Most of them said yes. Everyone likes to talk about themselves.

One of those women gave me the best negotiation advice I've ever heard. She said: "When you tell them the salary that you want, if they don't wince, the number isn't high enough."

Make them wince. (This could apply to your romantic life, too. It's up to you.)

KATE HARBIN CLAMMER

CEO, Source Capital

I led my first major company sale just a few years after my brother and I founded the private equity firm Source Capital. I was thirty-three years old and determined to not only be taken seriously, but to also be respected as a tough and skilled negotiator—not an easy feat in the male-dominated world of private equity.

The company's CEO, cofounder, and I all arrived early for the final sale negotiations on the fiftieth floor of a law office. As we waited in a large conference room, our conversation quickly escalated over the terms of their earn-outs. Suddenly, the two of them stormed out and did not return. I was horrified to be left alone.

We had so much riding on this deal, which was to be our "first exit." Our investors were counting on us. To make matters worse, the buyer group was about to arrive. We were already going to be outnumbered, but suddenly I realized it was going to be just me negotiating against a ten-man international team representing the corporate buyer. I went to the women's restroom to give myself a pep talk. Staring into the mirror, I told myself that I just had to stay calm and pretend like everything was fine. I knew it was vital that I not show any sign of weakness to the buyer.

Revealing nothing about what had just happened or offering any apologies for the absence of the company's management team, I successfully negotiated the terms and closed the deal.

Later we found out that the management walkout was a planned tactic to pressure us to give in to their demands. They gambled that we would postpone the meeting until their issues were resolved, but instead they lost their leverage when I continued on without them. While this sale was a critical first exit for Source Capital, handling it alone was, in many ways, just as important for me. This was the moment when I finally owned that I was not only the most powerful woman in the room, but also the most powerful person.

NORIA MORALES

Director of Design Partnerships, Target

This is not a typical negotiation "success story," but it's my own awakening. When I was offered a job at a large retail corporation, it came with a fancy title and a starting salary that was double what I was currently making as an editor for a media company. I was so blown away by the massive increase I didn't even think to negotiate it—against the advice of my husband, who encouraged me to push for an even higher starting salary. I was afraid the employer might get angry and pull the deal, because in my mind, negotiation had a negative ring to it. I accepted the offer, thrived in my role, and started paying attention to my value.

Six years later, I'm far more confident and self-aware of the unique expertise and experience I could bring to a company, and I have a better hold of industry standards. Most importantly, I know what matters to *me* and *my* life (it's way more than just the starting salary). Don't negotiate because someone tells you that you should. Negotiate only with the full confidence and understanding of your capabilities, experience, and the value you will bring. That takes preparation and work, but the result is organic negotiation that you initiate *for you*.

THE MOST
POWERFUL
WOMAN
IN THE
ROOM . . .

4

grows stronger
every time she fails

I f at first you don't succeed, try, try again. The person who came up with that showstopper missed the follow-up "and then after you try again, get up, dust yourself off, and keep on trying." Let's be honest: No one likes to lose. No one likes to be rejected. But the sooner you learn that rejection and failure are part of the game, the better equipped you will be to become the Most Powerful Woman in the Room. I believe you make your own destiny by being prepared for every opportunity that you seek out and using it to prove that you are the hardest worker in the room. I also know from experience that even if you give it your all, sometimes it doesn't work out the way you want it to work out. The Most Powerful Woman in the Room doesn't let that stop her from going after what she wants. She uses failure as a learning tool to help her grow, sharpen her skills, and pivot in a new direction. You never know what opportunity that failure will bring or how it will open a door that you didn't even see because you were so focused on the intended outcome. Be open to everything. Understand that being in second or third place or in some cases never achieving a particular goal may be teaching you a valuable lesson you can use to get where you want, taking a different path from how you first thought you would get there.

After leaving my small town and even smaller private school in Louisiana at the age of thirteen to attend boarding school at the prestigious Taft School in Connecticut, I felt like I had entered an alternate universe. From the moment I stepped onto the picturesque campus, resplendent with rolling hills covered in trees that were already showing signs of fall, almost everything about the school seemed new and unfamiliar. I had arrived early for preseason to play field hockey, a sport I had never heard of, with a roommate from Hong Kong, a place I knew almost nothing about, with classmates from places like New York City and Greenwich who seemed light-years ahead of me both socially and academically. It was daunting at best. It wasn't until a few weeks into my freshman semester that I finally saw something that felt familiar. At Vespers, an all-school assembly one evening before dinner, Hydrox, the school's female a cappella singing group, belted out a song that gave me full-body chills. I have loved singing my whole life, having grown up singing in our church choir every Sunday from a very early age, as well as any score from the cassettes my mom played in the car from musicals being performed in the West End or on Broadway. I could already visualize myself onstage with Hydrox, dressed in all black, harmonizing and belting out popular songs. All I could think was, *Please, God, get me up there.* The mostly upper-school women in this group seemed like everything I wanted to be. Onstage, in charge, singing, dressed up . . . what could I do to make this happen? It seemed to me that everyone was transfixed, watching their every move—or maybe that was just me. Whatever I had seen, I knew that it was definitely something I wanted to be part of as soon as possible.

When I saw the tryout sheet, I felt like it had been written for me and only me. I enthusiastically jotted down all the notes that I would need to be ready for the big day. The sheet mentioned that each candidate would be expected to prepare a song for tryouts, which would take place over a two-day period. I spent the rest of the week rehearsing the song in my room. I am pretty sure my roommate, for whom English was a second language, hadn't been intimately familiar with the lyrics to "I Dreamed a Dream" from *Les Misérables* and was my solo audience for at least an hour or two of in-room rehearsal. The following week, I sat nervously with a group of girls, mostly older than I was, waiting for the members of Hydrox to start the tryouts.

Now flash back to your freshman year in high school, when you truly believe the juniors and seniors are a different species of human. Passing by one of these creatures in the hallway, I would allow myself just enough time for a quick glance to see if I could pick up any fashion tips or hear a snippet of their conversation. It felt more than a little surreal to think girls who at that point had barely acknowledged my existence were actually speaking *to me*. The tryout instructions were simple; we would each sing a song to the group on our own and then they would integrate us into the group to see if we could harmonize. One by one we sang our song for the group. When my name was called, my knees felt like jelly, but I still felt confident when I sang "I Dreamed a Dream." After everyone had a chance to perform their song, they called us back in smaller groups to let us sing with the full group. Years of singing in school and church choirs had finally paid off. I easily read the music, harmonized with the other girls, and felt totally comfortable. I was mentally checking off the people who would be cut—the girl who was so nervous she was bright red with a shaky voice the entire tryout, the girl who was perpetually off-key throughout the entire session, the girl who had flubbed her lines during the initial tryout. I actually felt sad after the first day of try-outs ended, as I had enjoyed it so much. I spent most of the night in my room with a knot in my stomach promising God a number of things in return for helping me make it to the next round.

By the time the bell rang to indicate first period was over, the list had been posted.

I practically ran down the hall and shoved people out of the way as I scanned down the short list in alphabetical order—my name was there!

The group had gone from fifteen to five, and sitting at the top of the alphabetical list was Lydia Fenet. I was beyond elated.

Two days later, the five of us sat in the music room again as the members of Hydrox explained the final day of tryouts. All five of us would be singing with the group as if we were in one of their own rehearsals. They handed out music, lined us up according to vocal range, and the tryouts started. The whole thing probably lasted an hour, but to me it felt way too short. I was completely in my element, singing away and having a blast. At the end of the hour, the head of Hydrox thanked us all for our time and told us the final list would be posted the next day.

Again, a night of tossing and turning, and pledges to give away my earthly possessions in last-ditch prayers to God. As the sun rose, I was still awake, nervously excited to find my name posted on the board for everyone to see.

In today's world, if you are receiving important information, you are likely receiving it in an email. I rarely even pause to think about it because it is such a normal part of our everyday life. But if you do stop to think about it, you should feel lucky, because when you receive news—good or bad—in an email, you can open it whenever you want, wherever you want. If the news is good, you can run to find people to share it with. If the news is bad, you can disappear for a while until you are ready to put on a game face and find people to connect with about the unfortunate outcome. On the opposite end of the spectrum, you have what I had to deal with: a final list that is posted on a public bulletin board for two full days in the middle of the main hallway of school. A list on a bulletin board forces you to confront your emotions with witnesses all around you. There is no hiding.

After breakfast, I walked by the bulletin board, trying to act casual as I threw a quick glance at it. No list. Bell rings, first period begins, bell rings, first period ends. I dart from my desk and run to the board, palms sweating. *Argh.* Again, nothing. Class after class, bell after bell, until finally, as the last class of the day lets out and I run back to the bulletin board, there it is. The list is up. But instead of running, I feel myself slowing to a walk as I approach the board.

HYDROX FINALISTS

Two names.

Neither of them is mine.

I am sure that everyone reading this book has felt this feeling at some point. The feeling of shock, disbelief, numbness. You feel as if time has stopped. I wish I could tell you that I looked at the list, shrugged it off, and walked away; that I am immune to disappointment and rejection. I didn't and I'm not. I stood staring at the list with tears pricking my eyes. Surely there was a mistake. But as the crowd gathered to check out the various notices on the board, I heard a yelp of excitement as one of the juniors who had made the final cut leapt up and hugged her boyfriend, and I realized that no amount of time staring at the list was going to change the outcome. I slinked back to my room, cried for the next couple of hours, and then went upstairs to use the pay phone to call my mom. Also, I ate a pound of M&M's. Some moments in life call for chocolate.

Is there anything as painful as wanting something so badly that you feel like you can will it to happen and then realizing that there is nothing you can do? After many, many boxes of Kleenex and a couple of days spent moping around with my friends, I decided to move on and focus on other things. About a week after the list came out, I was walking down a hallway between classes when I heard someone call my name. I turned around to see one of the seniors whom I had briefly met during the Hydrox tryouts.

"Hey, I just wanted to tell you that you had a really great audition the other day. We were really impressed with your singing. You would have been a great fit, but the other girl that we chose has been trying out for three years and this was her last chance. Definitely try out again next year—there is no question that you will make it."

And just like that, my faith in the universe was restored. I knew that I belonged in Hydrox. I knew it to my core. It was just timing. It would all work out as I knew it would; it would only take a year longer than I had hoped.

Luckily for me, another singing group, a choir called Collegium, hosted tryouts not long after Hydrox. This time when the bell rang and I ran to the board, my name sat proudly at the top of the Collegium list of new sopranos. I was elated. The sharp sting of rejection from Hydrox had been replaced by the excitement of joining Collegium. Besides, I now knew there was a place waiting for me in Hydrox next year. Although at times I was jealous as I watched Hydrox perform at Parents' Weekend, at school meetings, and at key school gatherings throughout the year, it felt easy to temper these feelings knowing that by sophomore year I would be onstage singing with the group.

When the tryout announcement for Hydrox was posted the following September, it was my time. I scribbled down the date and time of the audition in my binder and walked excitedly to my next class. Aside from the fact that my voice had been a little scratchy that morning, I was fully confident that it would be cleared up for the tryout two days later. Boy, was I wrong. Instead of clearing up, my voice went away. As in, disappeared. By the time I arrived for tryouts in a room filled with people I knew, I could barely eke out the notes for the song. My saving grace was that the women in the room knew I could sing, so they invited me back for the second round in hopes that my voice would be restored. But when I woke up with absolutely no voice on the second day of tryouts, even I knew the chances of making Hydrox that year were slim to none.

I knew I didn't make the cut before I even saw the list on the board; yet it didn't soften the blow. There were tears, M&M's, you know the drill. And again, there was nothing I could do except wait another year and try again.

And so I waited until the following September. When the tryout announcement was posted, I didn't need to jot down the audition details. I could have written the announcement by that point. The next day I filed into the music room and sat among a group of friends and peers as they discussed how the tryouts would take place. I sang my song, I harmonized with the group, and two days later I attended the callbacks. This time I knew not to sprint to the board after each class. I waited until the final bell from the final class of the day rang and then walked cautiously to the board, my body anticipating the full blow of rejection, based on my last two experiences.

HYDROX FINALISTS

Lydia Fenet

I saw only one name. Mine. I am sure there were others, but in that moment, it was the only one that mattered to me.

Sometimes I think the high of getting what you want can be even higher when you have experienced the low of rejection. After two years of waiting and hoping, it had finally happened, and I savored the moment when I was the one who stood in front of the bulletin board and hugged my friends. But I also hugged the girl standing beside me who didn't make the cut because I knew what that felt like as well. Your moment of euphoria can also be a moment of pure sadness for someone else. And I sure knew what she was feeling in that moment.

Hydrox was everything I wanted it to be and more, but I often wonder if it would have been the same if I had been accepted on the first try. I can tell you that I didn't squander a minute of that opportunity. I enjoyed every rehearsal, every friendship, and certainly every performance. That experience taught me the bitterness of disappointment, but also the sweetness of overcoming that disappointment and never giving up.

As with so many life lessons I have learned along the way, I find part of me is glad I experienced those failures and rejections, because when inevitably something doesn't go my way, it doesn't feel as daunting. It certainly wasn't the last time I felt the wind knocked out of me: when I found out I didn't get into my first choice for college, when I found out that someone else got a promotion instead of me, when I found out that someone who told me she wanted to be my roommate decided she was going to move out of the city and left me scrambling for a new place to live. Each and every one of these moments taught me that rejection does not define me. In fact, having had these types of "character building" experiences, as my parents would call them, taught me not to crumble when something unexpected blindsides me in my personal or professional life. I know to take the time to sit out for a while, accept the disappointment, and try again. This often leads me to use a different approach that could be more effective than the one I tried in the first place.

About a month after I started strategic partnerships, I received a call from our president telling me that Christie's had won the right to sell the estate of Elizabeth Taylor, which included one of the most extraordinary jewelry collections that had ever come to market—and probably ever will. At the time, I knew very little of Elizabeth Taylor other than what I had seen in *People* magazine. I had no idea her relationship with Richard Burton had captivated the imagination of the world in a way that could be compared only to the Angelina Jolie–Brad Pitt story of today.

Christie's was selected to handle the sale of the collection with a global tour starting in Moscow in September. It was June. Our president told me that to amplify the marketing campaign they were looking for significant sponsorship funding of over $1 million in order to showcase the collection to the broadest global audience. Here I was with my new department, my global remit, and the pressure was on. It was one of the most challenging periods of my career—I was a department of one person, splitting my assistant with my old events team, and I was supposed to find millions of dollars in sponsorship from companies all around the world. Sleepless nights much? I needed a strategy, fast.

I decided to take the same approach I took when training for my first marathon or writing this book. Focus on 1 mile, not 26.2 miles; write 1,000 words a day, don't think about writing 70,000 words. Instead of focusing on the enormity of the sponsorship amount needed for a tour of this size, and given the short lead time that I had to find the money, I decided to approach companies to see if I could secure either an overarching sponsor for the whole tour or smaller sponsors per region. To start off, I reached out internally to our international specialists for any leads and contacts they thought might be helpful. Then, I focused on creating individual pitches that would entice these companies into parting with their sponsorship dollars to partner with Christie's for this historic sale. I spent long days and even longer nights working and reworking my pitch for every type of potential partner. I would speak to banks about engaging their top clients with an opportunity to view Elizabeth Taylor's 33-carat ring in a private setting. I would speak to fashion brands about her trendsetting styles and made sure to reach out to companies that she'd had close relationships with, like Valentino and Halston. I would speak with oil and gas companies in Russia about God only knows what. The point was for me to prove that my business plan would work: Christie's could leverage its greatest asset—the brand—and create an additional revenue stream within the company.

Even in the earlier days when I didn't have a single contract signed or penny confirmed, I kept my poker face intact to instill confidence in those around me. I will never forget when Wells

Fargo called to say it was on board to sponsor our entire Los Angeles exhibition. This idea that I had pushed so hard to move forward was going to work.

After signing the contract for Wells Fargo and a few other major sponsors, a colleague suggested that I reach out to a well-known company in Asia that was interested in hosting an exhibition stop as a client-engagement opportunity. Excited at the prospect of bringing in a sponsor with very deep pockets, I found the email address of the chief marketing officer through another contact and reached out immediately. Shortly thereafter, I received an email from his assistant with a request for a call later that evening. Since he was thirteen hours ahead of New York, I had ample time to pull together a proposal in anticipation of the call. It could not have gone better if I had scripted it. After that enthusiastic call with the chief marketing officer, I sent along a detailed proposal outlining the financial terms and expectations for a brand association with such a prominent global exhibition.

That evening when I went to bed, I fully expected that he would review the proposal and email back his offer so we could begin negotiations on the sponsorship amount. It is certainly what I would have done! To my delight, I woke up the next morning to an email from the chief marketing officer committing at the financial level I had outlined and asking for further details about the marketing and public relations strategy. When you are creating customized exhibitions and traveling across the world with hundreds of thousands of dollars of jewelry, there is a lot of red tape that has to be worked through. As the timing for this exhibition was sandwiched between two other tour stops, the timeline for making it happen was getting shorter by the day.

But first. THE CELEBRATION. After jumping up and down

around my bedroom, yelping with excitement, I fired off an email to the entire team with the news! Not only would we have the opportunity to expand the scope of the tour to a location with potential clients, but I had brought in a sponsor who would provide the rest of the money needed to fund the tour. Money raised. Job well done. Feeling like a superstar, I walked into the team meeting the next morning to high fives from my colleagues and even higher praise from our president, for whom I had the utmost respect.

For the first few days after the agreement to sponsor a new tour stop, the chief marketing officer and I would speak every evening, ending the call around 11:00 p.m. Following our call, I would send an email update to the necessary team members so that everyone was clear about what was needed to make this project happen. While this was taking place, our legal team drafted a contract that I sent to the CMO along with wiring instructions for the full amount of the sponsorship to be paid in full upon signing the contract. As the exhibition was taking place in a little over a month, I asked that the money be wired within the next two weeks to ensure that we were on track to bring the jewels. He agreed to the terms over email and said he would be in touch shortly with the contract.

What a STAR, you must be thinking.

But come on, people. This is a chapter on overcoming rejection, so you must have expected that there was going to be some adversity along the way.

The next morning I sent an email to the CMO requesting a call so that I could update their team on the exhibition plans and marketing strategy for the tour stop. Work was insanely busy, so I didn't think anything about the fact that I didn't receive a reply. In fact, that evening I remember feeling relieved that I could go to bed before 11:00 p.m., the time that our calls would typically wind down each night. I was a little surprised the next morning that I didn't have an email with any additional information, but at the same time I figured he was probably busy and would get back to me when he had a chance. The Christie's team was getting a little anxious because they needed answers in order to create the exhibition layout, but I assured them that everything was fine. Because it was, wasn't it?

The following morning, however, when my emails and requests for calls continued to go unanswered, I started to get an unsettled feeling in my stomach. Praying that I was being paranoid, I sent a "just checking in" email before I went to bed. But I spent the night tossing and turning. I couldn't shake the feeling that something was wrong. After finally falling asleep between three and four o'clock in the morning, I jolted awake only a couple of hours later and immediately grabbed my phone. I closed my eyes hoping that when I opened them there would be an email with an attached signed contract and confirmation of the wire transfer sitting at the top of my inbox. Alas, no. Radio silence. Morning after morning. I would stare at my phone in disbelief and then duck into my office at work, doing my best to avoid anyone from the team who would ask for a status update.

After seven of the longest days of my life, I finally received an email. It just wasn't the email I wanted to receive. The email was brief; they weren't going to be able to participate in the tour. Full stop. No explanation, no "I'm sorry for taking you on this ride." Just a big old N-O. Perhaps you are thinking that the worst part of this was the fact that we didn't get the money. I'll admit, that was pretty painful. But the worst part was having to go into the meeting later that day and tell my colleagues who had been giving me high fives that we weren't getting the money and we weren't going to exhibit in that country. I felt like such a failure, and worse, I felt like I had let them all down.

What you need to realize as the Most Powerful Woman in the Room is that the stakes only get higher the more successful you are in life. The higher you go, the farther you have to fall. But trust me when I say that the view gets better and better the higher you go. What matters more than the failure (no matter how successful you are, it's going to happen at some point) is what you do in the direct aftermath. Ultimately my original strategy of finding more sponsors at lower levels was the one that brought me to the target goal for the exhibition; it wasn't the big win that I had hoped for, but reaching a goal is reaching a goal no matter how you hit it. My colleagues were always supportive and even gave me a second round of high fives when I announced that I had hit my target . . . this time with a signed contract in hand so that there was no question that the money was coming in.

The most important thing is that you learn from each experience instead of letting it stop you in your tracks. In the case of the missing CMO, I learned to wait until a contract is signed before confirming anything to my team. I learned to be transparent if I think that things are going wrong on a deal, so that the final outcome is not such a surprise. And most of all, I learned that as long as you are trying your best, you will still have the respect of your peers.

Perhaps the greatest training ground for overcoming a fear of rejection is the auction stage. It makes a couple of failed attempts at Hydrox, and the loss of a major sponsorship deal, look inconsequential. I guess you could say that I have been forced to be good at rejection since I am rejected numerous times whenever I get onstage. And in some cases, it is a room filled with as many as 5,600 people.

Every year for the past couple of years, I have taken an auction for the Bob Woodruff Foundation at Madison Square Garden. For those of you who aren't familiar with the Hulu Theater at Madison Square Garden in New York City, I will tell you one thing: it seats 5,600 people. In the context of this story, that is really all you need to know. Every year the Bob Woodruff Foundation hosts a star-studded event called Stand Up for Heroes in the week leading up to the New York Comedy Festival. Stand Up for Heroes raises money for the Bob Woodruff Foundation, which supports veterans in readjusting to their new lives with serious physical impairments. In our initial call the first year that I agreed to take the auction, they informed me that I would go onstage following comedy acts by Jon Stewart, John Oliver, and Jim Gaffigan for a brief paddle raise. Following the paddle raise, Bruce Springsteen would play a set and then I would go back onstage and auction off his guitar.

With him. The Boss. Bruce Springsteen himself.

And then all the comedians and I would come back onstage and we would auction off a motorcycle with Bruce Springsteen. Together.

So, yeah. This was definitely going to be a little different from my average Tuesday. Or any Tuesday in my life. Ever.

Once I had regained my composure on the call, we started discussing levels for the paddle raise. It is the moment when everyone in the room is encouraged to raise their paddle to give money to the organization. Unlike the live auction, you don't end up with an exotic vacation or a priceless experience or a puppy. You are simply raising your hand with a paddle and giving money.

I always like to have a frank conversation with nonprofits about the first level that I am asking for during the paddle raise. It is important that I set the right tone for the paddle raise by ensuring there is someone who can and wants to give at the highest level.

After our initial call, based on the previous year's auction, we agreed that I would start off the paddle raise at $100,000, and then take the requests down from there. So later that week, after flashing my all-access pass and sitting in the green room as the audience filled the massive auditorium, my "handler" came to escort me down to stage left, where all the talent was waiting to do their set onstage. I made my way in the darkly lit area to a chair where I could see the profiles of the comedians about to go on: Jon Stewart, John Oliver, and Jim Gaffigan. I sat in a folding chair toward the back of the staging area as each of them performed his fifteen-minute set—I spent much of the time alternating between laughing loudly and nervously twisting my gavel over and over in my palm as we got closer and closer to the paddle raise. When the video about the Bob Woodruff Foundation began to roll, I took my microphone from the stagehand and moved into position in the wings of Madison Square Garden.

At the time I took this auction I had probably taken around 1,200 auctions in venues of every shape and size. A hundred people at a dinner? Fifteen hundred people at a dinner? You've seen one ballroom, you've seen them all. But as I took my position between the velvet drapes in the wings, I remember thinking, *Now THAT is a lot of people.*

"3, 2, 1 . . ." I strode purposefully across the long stage toward the small music stand that was placed in the middle of the stage in lieu of a podium. I put my notes down and banged my gavel three times against the tiny music stand, which made a small tinny *ting, ting, ting* sound instead of the loud BANG, BANG, BANG that I usually get from the podium. Kind of awkward, but it was what it was.

The Strike engaged, I felt confident, gave a huge smile, and launched into my description leading up to the paddle raise. My last line leading into the paddle-raise ask is clear: "This is the opportunity for everyone in the room to give back to our wounded veterans who have given so much to our country. Who in this audience will start off our paddle raise with a $100,000 gift for our wounded heroes?"

And as I always do with a paddle raise, I give it a little time to let anyone who likes to hold back on the bidding for a dramatic flair get ready for their big moment. And then I give it another ten seconds because everyone was confident that there was someone who wanted to give at that level. And then another ten seconds just in case that person fell asleep and someone is trying to wake him up and remind him that he is supposed to be raising his hand. And then another ten seconds because Bruce Springsteen is waiting in the wings less than ten feet away . . .

Nothing.

Are you dying a little inside right now imagining this scenario? Standing onstage in front of an audience of 5,600 people staring up at you while uncomfortably shifting in their seats. Because I was definitely dying. Truly. DYING. But you know what? At the end of the day, whatever I get in a paddle raise is more than the organization had before I started, so I have to keep the energy high, keep a smile on my face, and show everyone that I am the Most Powerful Woman in the Room. I am the one who sets the tone, and the audience feeds off that energy. I waited a few more seconds on the off chance that my mystery bidder decided to do a last-minute run to the bar . . . and when I was absolutely positive this mystery bidder was not going to raise their hand, then I gave everyone a huge smile and said with a wink:

"Well, you know, a girl's gotta ask!"

Because you know what? YOU HAVE TO ASK. The worst thing that someone can say is no. And lucky for you, it probably won't be in front of 5,600 people.

Rejection? Not going to slow me down.

I quickly pivoted to $50,000, and two bidders immediately raised their hands.

You will be happy to know that the rest of the evening was a huge success. Bruce Springsteen and I . . . I'll say that again, because I can rarely make a statement that begins like this . . . Bruce Springsteen and I sold his guitar, a ride on his motorcycle, and a tray of his mom's lasagna for $370,000. At the last minute, he decided to double the lot. As I drove up the bidding between two bidders, Bruce leaned over at the last minute and whispered into my ear, "Sell it twice," meaning he was donating another guitar, ride on his motorcycle, and, yes, another tray of his mom's lasagna to the underbidder for $370,000 on the spot. $740,000 raised in five minutes. After Bruce played a set, I went back onstage with all the comedians to sell a motorcycle (that retailed for $12,000) for $100,000—all for veterans. It was an amazing night all around, and despite the fact that it had started out with a moment of rejection, the end result surpassed all our expectations.

Did I mention that I was onstage with Bruce Springsteen?

Failure and rejection are treated with kid gloves these days. The Most Powerful Woman in the Room understands that the gloves are off when it comes to learning how to overcome feelings of rejection and failure in order to move forward and keep going. The next time you feel utter despair when you don't get something you thought you couldn't live without, know that you can live without it and the fact that you didn't get it is part of what will truly make you stronger. The Most Powerful Woman in the Room can and will get over rejection because she understands that even if it doesn't yield the result she wants, she can use it as a learning tool and grow from the experience. She understands that she needs to embrace rejection and turn it into her biggest strength. It is hard to fail, hard to hear the word no, painful to be rejected, but do not let that fear stop you from trying for the outcome that YOU want.

a time when things didn't go their way

BARBARA CORCORAN

**Real Estate Mogul,
Shark Tank Investor, and Podcast Host**

Right after I signed the contract to be on a new show called *Shark Tank*, the producer announced he had changed his mind and was giving the lone female seat to someone else. Rather than accepting the defeat, I sat down at my computer and banged out a list of things I had succeeded at once someone told me I couldn't. I ended the email with, "All the best things in my life happened on the heels of failure and I consider your rejection a lucky charm." I suggested he invite both women out to compete for the seat. The next week, I booked a flight to LA and got the job. I've been a very happy investor on *Shark Tank* for ten years and just renewed my contract.

DEBORAH ROBERTS

Award-Winning Correspondent, ABC News

Early in my television career, like any other budding reporter, I screwed up big-time. As an intern at WMAZ-TV in Macon, Georgia, I was often sent on assignments with the reporters to help shoot and later edit their stories. One afternoon I was asked to help out with a shoot at Fort Benning, the nearby army base. My job was to carry the camera deck and press the start and stop button.

We hustled through the woods and found moments to interview commanders about the training. It was a long but exciting day. That is, until we got back to the edit room and discovered I had pressed the stop button when we were filming, and pressed the start button when we weren't. We had lots of shots of feet and grass . . . and black silence when we had hoped to have an interview. I wanted to crawl under the desk. After a few moments of stony disbelief, the other reporter stormed out of the edit room. She didn't speak to me for a while and I went home in tears, convinced that I would be shown the door. After a pep talk from my mom, I came back to work the next day, apologetic and eager to help. I put on a brave face as my heart pounded. And to my surprise, the reporter had calmed down and suggested that we reschedule.

We were granted a weekend reshoot, and days later we were back at it. I carried the bulk of the massive gear and paid close attention to every detail. After our unintentional trial run days before, this shoot was easier and actually slightly better. The reporter and I bonded over the experience and later—much later—even laughed about it. Mistakes will happen even with the best of intentions. But what matters most is getting back up and trying again.

THE MOST
POWERFUL
WOMAN
IN THE
ROOM . . .

5

harnesses the power of community

I dragged my oversize suitcase up a flight of stairs into a studio apartment fresh out of college at the age of twenty-one. The friendships that I had carefully cultivated over four magical years at Sewanee, a small liberal arts college in Tennessee, vanished overnight as I moved to a city where I knew almost no one. My first years were busy but lonely, and despite the energy and bustle of the people outside my door, I desperately longed for the days that I spent surrounded by a community of friends who were readily available to delve into the topic of the moment no matter what time of day or night. I craved that sense of community so much that I began to create it—collecting new friends and contacts at every opportunity so that now, twenty years after I arrived, New York feels like a small town despite the fact that it is home to millions of people.

Those formative years in New York taught me something that I am reminded of daily: there is nothing as powerful as community. My community plays a huge part in my life as a working mom with three small children. I lean on my community of friends and family every day, from my coworkers, who offer to cover a last-minute meeting if I need to be home to take my child to a doctor's appointment; to a mom friend who takes my son to soccer after school so that our nanny can pick up my daughter at the bus stop; to my parents, in-laws, and siblings, who are always available to help out with the children if my husband and I are traveling. Everywhere I turn I see this type of engagement and interaction among my female friends. We are the core of our communities. We spend our days juggling personal lives, enriching our communities, raising families, starting companies, running companies, looking for our next step. In each of these roles, we strive to make connections, create new platforms, and gain a deeper understanding of something that interests us. But even though we are the ones making those connections, very few women I know feel comfortable selling, which, given the role that we play within our communities, you would think would be a natural next step. Right? Well . . . no.

If you are like many women I know, selling something—whether it is a product or your vision—makes you feel uncomfortable. It feels unnatural, a little showy, or maybe it feels like you are bragging. Women who sell are often made to feel like there is something shameful in selling to make a living or earn your own money. Society makes us feel that selling or sales is a negative thing, at odds with the natural tendency of most women to be deferential to a more aggressive salesperson or a louder voice in the room. My incredibly talented mother started a handbag line after all her kids left for college, and she used to tell me over and over again, "I am always happy to sell something that someone else made, but I am just the worst salesperson for my purses because I feel like when they say no, they are rejecting me, not the purse." No matter how many times my dad, my siblings, and I would try to dissuade her of this notion, she couldn't shake the feeling. I have heard this same phrase throughout my time as an auctioneer: *I could never do what you do when you are onstage; I am so bad at asking people for things.*

It certainly isn't a generational thing, nor, as I originally assumed having grown up in the South, is it a southern thing. A friend of mine in New York who started a children's clothing company confided to me over dinner that she overheard her friends talking about her when they thought she was out of earshot. She felt stunned and embarrassed when she heard one of them say, "Well, you know how she is always peddling her wares." She mentioned it casually, but I could tell that it had upset her to her core. She was proud of her business and what she was building after her first job as a stay-at-home mom to three kids. What she overheard her friend say made her question that pride, which made no sense to me—she was simply hustling to build her business. Whenever I encounter this type of situation in my life or someone shares a story like this with me, I always take a step back and think about why someone would make a comment like that. Even if it wounds me, I know deep down that the people who say things to intentionally hurt other people are often projecting their own insecurities or jealousy. So instead of feeling embarrassed when someone makes a comment like that, I try to have empathy for a person who feels threatened by someone else's success. Clearly they have a void in their life that isn't being filled and they are using negativity to fill it. Why would anyone try to tear you down when you are building something up?

Easy for me to say, right? I won't pretend that I haven't felt just as upset when I heard things that have been said about me. I had a similar moment years ago when a colleague mentioned that she had worked at Sotheby's, Christie's main competitor in the auction world, for a few years prior to coming to Christie's. She relayed a story of how my name came up in one of their senior executive meetings and someone in the meeting had said cattily, "Well, Lydia is really good at selling herself." When she relayed the story, I felt my face flush red and wished that the floor would open and swallow me whole. I am sure that, as you read this, you feel a little embarrassed for me. What a self-promoter, right? Over that week and the weeks that followed, I replayed that sentence over and over in my head. I felt ashamed that I had been called out in a public forum for promoting myself, for believing that I deserved to be acknowledged for years and years of hard work. I was embarrassed that other people saw me as a promoter of me.

How I wish I could travel back to that day and shake that version of me. What I should have said was, "Thank you. Best compliment I have received in a long time."

You know what? The person who said that was right. I am good at selling myself. I am so good at selling myself that I am writing a book to help other people learn how to do it and do it well. There is no shame in being good at selling. And more importantly, there is no shame in selling yourself, your vision, or something you built or created. No one will ever know your strengths and weaknesses as well as you do. You are uniquely qualified to sell yourself and your vision to other people. The next time you feel that twinge of self-doubt when you are pushing for yourself, remember that the Most Powerful Woman in the Room gets what she wants because she goes after it full throttle. She writes her own dialogue and creates her own story line. A truly powerful woman doesn't do it by putting other people down; she does it by lifting people up, and benefits from that act as much as driving herself to live up to her fullest potential. There will always be people who won't be able to handle your success, and frankly you don't need them to believe in you. Because starting today, you are going to be your biggest supporter and believer in you; everyone else can get on board or find another plane. Because your plane is going to be filled with other people you have motivated and inspired along the way. The community of people you have surrounded yourself with and spent time building and cultivating.

I often find myself starting a sentence with, "And, as you know, everything in my life comes back to a story about charity auctioneering . . ." Because so often in my life, I realize that a narrative that I have seen take shape in my own life can also be applied to selling. I have learned that people respond to selling when it connects them to a larger vision and makes them feel like they are part of positive, forward movement. People want to feel part of something larger than themselves. And many years into charity auctioneering, I recognized that this need for authenticity and connection could be leveraged into an incredibly effective selling technique.

When I first started taking auctions, I dreaded the paddle raise, as did most of my colleagues. One minute the guests are engaged in frenetic bidding as they try to win the luxury vacation of a lifetime, and the next minute you are asking them to bid . . . on nothing. It can make even the most entertaining auction feel like air slowly being let out of a balloon.

After many, *many* long, painful paddle raises, I decided that I had to figure out a better strategy. The paddle raise always felt like a yearly dental checkup—something that everyone dreaded but agreed had to be done. I was tired of watching the audience completely engaged for the first part of the auction only to turn their backs on me and drown me out as I transitioned from the auction to the paddle raise. Moreover, in many cases the paddle raise had the potential to make more money than the live portion of the auction simply because of the number of people in the room, but it never did because people stopped paying attention the minute the live auction was over. Even worse, sometimes there was no auction; it was just the paddle raise. Ten years into my auctioneering career, I hated feeling like I had mastered the auction but still couldn't make the paddle raise exciting or interesting. After many failed and flat paddle raises, I realized that I was missing something in my selling technique. I was approaching the paddle raise as a chance for individuals to give money. The crowd was lacking one thing, and it certainly wasn't cocktails. It was unity. They were being asked to give as individuals, and the person raising their hand to give the highest number would look just as sheepish as the person giving at the lowest number. Those giving the most at the top felt guilty about having so much to give in a public forum, whereas those at the bottom felt embarrassed that they couldn't give more.

Charity galas in New York typically stop after Memorial Day and start up again after Labor Day, so I usually have the summer off to rest up before it all begins again. During my three-month break from the auction stage, I strategized about what I could do to make the paddle raise less painful and more fun. At that point the bar was so low that I was certain it could not have been any more painful. In a room of 500 people there will be a number of individuals who can give a ton and a few who can only give $5, but the other 480 people in the room can probably give somewhere north of $20. As I always say to the nonprofits, $20 is more than you had before you started. The more I thought about it, the more I was convinced that what I was missing in the paddle raise was not the potential bidders; it was the audience working together as a community rather than a group of individual donors raising their paddles.

Every year in New York, the black-tie gala season kicks off with a benefit for New Yorkers for Children. It has become one of the most anticipated events over the years, with top philanthropists from New York as well as celebrities such as Beyoncé and Jay-Z sitting at the head table. New Yorkers for Children is an incredible organization that aims to help at-risk youths in or aging out of foster care through education, career development, lessons on life skills, and work with the Administration for Children's Services. I have worked with New Yorkers for Children as part of their Friends Committee for years, and I knew that they would trust me when I told them I wanted to try doing the paddle raise differently. Instead of simply asking people to give money when I called out a number, I asked them to give me a financial goal for the paddle raise. At that time, the goal for the paddle raise was a dream number that organizations were hoping to raise instead of a defined goal that the audience would have to stretch to achieve. The day before the auction, they finally settled on an amount: $250,000—it was more than they had made the year before, but it was what they needed to make in order to hit their revenue goal for the event. One thing they told me more than once: under no circumstances was I to tell the crowd the goal for the evening. What if we didn't reach it? What if they felt that the organization was being greedy? What if . . . What if . . . What if . . .

Roadblocks. We stand in front of them and let them intimidate us, right?

No.

The Most Powerful Woman in the Room hurdles them. One by one.

Onstage that evening there was no opportunity to warm up the crowd, as the organization had decided that we were going to do only a paddle raise, no live auction. I knew many of the people in the audience, and as I banged down my gavel, I also knew that they weren't going to stop talking for a simple paddle raise. This time, with a huge smile on my face, determined to show them that I was not backing down, I kept banging down my gavel, refusing to stop until I had their attention. Finally the crowd realized that I wasn't going to stop until they stopped talking. Once I had their attention, I told them the first thing that sprang to mind—if they could quiet down, I would let them in on a little secret. It is amazing how tricks that work with my three-year-old also work with a crowd of intoxicated grown-ups. The room went silent, with 500 pairs of eyes peering up at me from the barely lit ballroom.

"The organization told me specifically *not to tell you* what they need to hit their revenue goal. I swore to them that I would absolutely not tell you what the goal is for this paddle raise, because they are very worried that we are not going to reach it. But I am a goal-oriented person. So how can I come out here and not tell you what the goal is for this paddle raise? The goal is $300,000." A few people in the audience laughed out loud—I wasn't sure if they were laughing at the number or the fact that I had blatantly disobeyed a direct order from the organization. I kept on going with, "$300,000 is a huge amount of money, and I know that most of you don't think that we are going to hit the goal. But I want you to know that you guys are going to crush that number because there are 500 people in this room and every single one of you can give something. A paddle raise is simple. Just raise your paddle whenever I give you an amount that you feel comfortable donating to New Yorkers for Children. I will start at the highest level of giving and then go down to the least amount until we hit our goal. If we need to go down to a $10 paddle raise, I will do it, because I can't walk out of here without giving this organization what it needs to help the at-risk youth in this community. Dig deep, and then keep digging, because I am not getting off this stage until we are done."

Let's just say that the crowd could see that I was not going to be taking this paddle raise like the ones I had taken in the past.

"The organization has given me fifteen minutes for this paddle raise, but I say let's get it done in five. Put your wineglasses down, get ready to cheer for every single person who raises their hand, because we are going to blow right through our goal and keep on going."

With those words, I had changed the paddle raise from a moment that I used to dread into one that I was ready to rock. Giving the audience a challenge, challenging them to hit a number, setting a goal—it gave me a reason to be up there. And the audience? They were engaged, excited, and as ready to rise up to that challenge as I was to throw it down. They were no longer single donors raising their hands; they were a motivated group of people getting ready to reach their goal.

Without missing a beat, I used the energy that I felt emanating from the room to launch right into the paddle raise. Instead of simply calling out dollar amounts that I wanted people to give, starting at the highest number and moving to the lowest number, I gave examples of what the money would do for the organization so that people had a clear idea of how their money would help the nonprofit. The number $300,000 was our goal and this community of 500 people was going to make sure we hit it. For the children.

New Yorkers for Children told me to start the paddle raise asking for $25,000. Clearly, I was in the mood to hurdle roadblocks, so I started it off at $50,000—just in case there was someone who had made a little more that year than expected and felt like giving an insane amount of money. As luck would have it, someone *had* made a little extra that year and wasn't afraid to start us off at the highest level. All I had to do was ask and all of a sudden we had put a sizable dent in a very large goal. I showered compliments on our first donor, the crowd cheered, and we were off to the races.

"Thanks to our generous couple, who look like a younger, more successful version of Tom Brady and Gisele Bündchen, we only have $250,000 to go." Never underestimate the power of flattery in selling.

"You are the ones who are going to make this happen so let's keep going."

"Our next level of giving is $25,000, which will provide ten children with back-to-school packages giving them everything they need to succeed in their first year of college. Is there any brilliant, successful, hilariously funny man or woman who would like to donate at the $25,000 level?" Four donors raised their hands.

"And just like that, we only have $150,000 left to meet our goal." When the audience gave light applause, I demanded that they cheer for the donors who had cut our paddle-raise goal in half in less than a minute.

"Ladies and gentlemen, do you see how quickly I can be off the stage and you can be on the dance floor or getting your next cocktail? Let's keep this momentum going and crush this paddle raise."

The potential of me leaving the stage as well as the possibility of another drink fueled the energy in the room.

"Ten thousand dollars will purchase four more of the back-to-school packages for at-risk youth in foster care to provide them with essentials like comforters, computers, and transportation money for college."

Ten hands shot up, totaling $100,000, which meant that we'd raised $250,000 and had only $50,000 to go. Sensing that the momentum was carrying us rapidly to our goal, I swiftly moved on to the next level, keeping my energy level up and pushing the crowd to continue paying attention.

"Friends, we are getting dangerously close to the goal that you thought that we might not reach but I *knew* that you would. We have raised $250,000, and we only need $50,000. Let's finish this off here."

Down to the $5,000 level. "If we could get 10 people in this room to raise their hand at $5,000, we would hit our goal." Hands shot up rapidly but I could tell that we weren't quite there. I counted off the hands in rapid sequence, throwing in a joke here and there to keep people paying attention. Five hands in the air, another $25,000 to go.

There is always a point in the paddle raise when the energy starts to wane, when the counting of paddles and the buzz from cocktail hour start to wear off. Time to hit the accelerator and use every last drop of energy in my reserves.

"Okay, guys. We only have $25,000 to go. Only 18 people in this room have had a chance to give, but what incredible giving they have done. I am taking it down to the $1,000 level to see if we can get to our final goal of $300,000. Are you guys ready?"

Loud applause and cheering.

Again, hands flew up, and I counted them out loud.

"1, 2, 3, 4, 5, 6, 7, 8, 9 . . . We are at *$10,000*! KEEP IT COMING!"

I counted quickly and enthusiastically as we moved toward the final goal . . .

"11, 12, 13, 14, 15, 16, 17, 18, 19 . . ." I looked around the crowd furtively. We had only $6,000 to go until we hit the $300,000 goal, but there were no hands left in the air.

My head felt like it was going to explode from mentally tallying the numbers, but I knew how important it was that the audience knew how much more we needed to hit the goal.

"*Friends* . . ." I paused for dramatic effect. "Perhaps I should say BEST friends. We have come so far this evening . . . $294,000 far, in fact, and I think you can all agree that there is no way that I am getting off this stage unless we find the last $6,000. So I am going to add a final level at $500 because I know that 12 of out of the 500 people in this room will make this happen for these amazing kids. But before I ask, help me by cheering so loudly for the people who are about to give these gifts that they can hear us outside."

The audience started cheering—it was no longer a passive group, hoping that everyone else would give so the evening could move on. They were a unified group of people working together; every gift was important, no matter at what level.

"Here we go, guys. I'm counting from the left side to the right side of the room. Get your hands up.

"1, 2, 3, 4, 5, 6, 7, 8, 9, 10. TWO MORE TO GO!"

As we neared the goal, the energy in the room felt like a wave collecting more and more energy as it headed to shore. I could even feel it in my body as the adrenaline made my heart start racing. I could see members of the audience craning their necks to see if the final two hands carried us to the finish line. My voice cracked, and I could feel the lump in my throat as I saw the final two hands.

"11, 12 makes $300,000!!!"

It is so difficult to describe how important human connection and human emotion are when you are selling something, but I had just witnessed it firsthand. The audience responded to the goal that I set, the message that I relayed, and the desire to come with me on a journey to reach a goal. Near tears, I banged down the gavel and quickly exited the stage to more loud applause. The new executive director was waiting at the bottom of the stairs in tears herself.

The goal had actually been $250,000, but I knew that the people in the room could get us to $300,000 if I set a goal and took them along for the ride.

Selling to people takes a vision, it takes a story, and it takes a leader to bring a community of people along on that journey. Onstage taking the auctions, I am the Most Powerful Woman in the Room. But at any time in your life, in any room, it can be you. Because the Most Powerful Woman in the Room is a woman who knows how to effectively communicate herself and her message to a group of people. She is a woman who leads by example and shows those around her that there is strength in numbers, in those who choose to lift others up to lead with her. It is a woman who sets a goal, articulates that goal, and follows through; who understands that leadership is about the human connection, about inspiring and connecting not only by herself but encouraging other people to do it as well. There is an unbelievable amount of strength in numbers, in groups, in support, in connection. Connect, engage, inspire, and lead. The Most Powerful Woman in the Room doesn't need to have the loudest voice in the room because she has the conviction it takes to sell her vision. The Most Powerful Woman in the Room doesn't do it alone; she doesn't want to do it alone. She wants everyone to succeed as much as she wants to succeed. Strength in numbers. POWER in numbers. But most importantly, POWER in leadership.

THREE OTHER POWERFUL WOMEN ON . . .

finding their conviction and connection

MARY ALICE STEPHENSON

Founder and CEO, GLAM4GOOD

Shout it from the rooftops! People can't help you if they don't know what you need. Let people know in every way, every day, how important your work is to you and how and why they can and should support you! Remember, if you don't care, nobody else will. People can't get behind something if they don't understand and see it. Show them.

LAUREN BRODY

Author and Founder,
The Fifth Trimester Consulting

I came back to work after the birth of my first son feeling all kinds of wrecked by the experience until one day a junior colleague on my team thanked me, mid-meeting, for being so open about my struggle. Rather than scare her off, she said, I'd shown she could do it too one day, under-eye circles and all. That was a revelation. My success at work from that point on was never just about deliverables . . . it was about team building and mentoring a whole community of future working parents.

A few years in, I sold a proposal for a book to help women through what I called the Fifth Trimester, the return to work after baby. Very quickly, I learned the power of community again. I couldn't in good conscience rely only on my own—hard, but admittedly privileged—experience. I surveyed and interviewed eight hundred other new parents. Hourly wageworkers, single moms, and, yes, plenty of Fortune 500 execs too. As I analyzed the data and transcripts, the skeleton of my book emerged. I didn't have all the answers, but collectively, we sure did: these eight hundred women became one big "working-mom mentor" for the masses, spurring a whole Fifth Trimester movement and the most rewarding work of my life.

DEE POKU

Founder and CEO, Women Inspiration
& Enterprise

The secret to your success lies within your network, and no one ever succeeded without one. I was a classic worker bee, always first in and last out of the office. I truly believed that hard work and talent alone would get me to where I needed to be. And it does. It takes you far. But not if no one notices. Not if there's no one advocating for you in the corridors of power. It's important to have a strong group of allies who can make introductions, open doors, and help make your case. And it's never too late to start. Be a mentor to those coming up behind you, be an ally to your colleagues, and develop strong relationships with your boss and others in senior leadership. Make friends both within and outside your industry. Don't forget to ask, and then give as well as receive, and you'll see a seismic shift in the trajectory of your career. And always remember that when one woman rises, we all rise.

THE MOST POWERFUL WOMAN IN THE ROOM . . .

6

never misses an opportunity
to network

I grew up watching the king of all networkers work every room he entered, from the local coffee shop to a school basketball game to church on Sunday. If a doorman opened a door for my dad, they closed the door with his business card in their hand on the other side. Walking into any place that my father has visited once is like walking into a place that he has lived for fifty years; he already knows everyone in the place. I can remember looking through his stacks of binders in which some poor intern had spent countless weeks organizing his business card collection. Let's just say that everyone breathed a sigh of relief when Outlook came up with CONTACTS. If you were to ask my dad what the key to business success is, his answer would be simple: Network or Die.

Now, I am 99 percent sure that he was referring to one's *business* dying a slow death because no one is networking to bring in new clients. Not that I, personally, would die.

However, I wasn't taking any chances. So, when I started working, I took his advice.

Network I did. And network I do. And I will continue to network until I die.

So, let me pass the same advice along to you in a less fatalistic way.

You. Must. Network. Period.

Networking is, without a doubt, the most important, FREE— let me say that again, FREE—thing that you can do in your life. You probably don't realize that you already have a massive network. You have been building your network from the day you were born; every person you meet, every interaction you have, builds a network that can be utilized and maximized. Ultimately, it is how you cultivate and grow your network that will set you apart from every other person trying to sell. Because when it comes to selling, you are only as good as your network. But if you also know how to utilize other people's networks as well as your own, you can save yourself a lot of time going through LinkedIn.

Now, you are probably thinking exactly what I thought when I first started my career: *When you are just starting out, how do you get your foot in the door?*

How do you start building a network?

Once you are employed, how do you grow that network?

In the olden days, as I like to call the days before Google, building a network was a daunting experience. Some people were lucky—they already had access to potential employers, donors, and investors just because they went to the right school. Or perhaps they knew the right people or even grew up in a city where you could show up in the waiting room at an office and wait until someone important saw you. Realistically, back then, it wasn't until you had a face-to-face meeting and were holding on to a physical business card after having met a person that you could consider someone a part of your network. A person who did not have any of these advantages had a long road to face before they could track down someone in an industry that interested them, secure a business card, and get that meeting.

It is an entirely different ballgame now. We live in an age where information is a hotspot away. A quick Google search can yield the top ten companies or performers in any field. Websites like LinkedIn, Bumble Bizz, and Shapr provide you with access in the form of an email requesting a phone call or an email exchange with anyone from an intern at a company to a CEO. These sites make it easy by matching you with job opportunities that might be of interest based on your skill set and connections. In just five minutes you can identify and reach out to someone offering your dream job and use your carefully crafted Strike to set yourself apart from the hundreds of other emails that person probably receives a year from other interested candidates.

Let's say that you take the bull by the horns and come up with a winning Strike email that engages your targeted person, and they agree to a phone call or, even better, a meeting.

Pay attention to what I say next, because it seems obvious, but I can tell you from personal experience that people do not do this.

You *must* research the person you have asked to connect with before speaking with them. To include someone in your network, you need to stand out so that they remember you—and you want to stand out for the right reasons.

I cannot tell you how many informational interviews I have given where the person sitting across from me/calling me on the phone has no idea what I do. Moreover, they don't seem to know why they are calling me and have not spent any time preparing for the meeting. Half the time, after leaving these types of informational interviews, I can't even remember their name by the time I put down my phone or get back to my desk. So here are three tips to help you make a memorable impression:

1. *Take a call or walk into our meeting with a list of relevant questions.* Show me that you know what my company does and what I do in my role, and that you have spent more than two seconds researching what is happening in my field.

2. *Tell me in an articulate way what you have been busy doing up to this point in your life.* Give me an interesting anecdote or two that will help me remember you in future meetings (e.g., you just traveled across Europe and never want to stay in a hostel again; you grew up in a family with six siblings and therefore are very good at resolving conflicts; you love trying new restaurants but went to one last night and *do not* go there because you saw a mouse).

3. *Be efficient with your time and with my time.* Show up a few minutes early so that the meeting starts when it is supposed to start. Be cognizant of the time scheduled for the meeting so that you can wrap it up in the allotted time with a final question. If I am enjoying the conversation, I will always extend it, but it is nice to know that someone is aware of the fact that I may have another meeting directly after ours.

The Most Powerful Woman in the Room does her homework before emailing, taking a meeting, or making a call when she is networking. She should know as much as she possibly can about the company and the person she is contacting, and should even have an agenda set for the cold call that she is making that shows she is prepared, efficient, and respectful of others' time.

For those of you who are lucky enough to attend a school with a robust alumni program, utilize their services. If not, use other resources on the internet like LinkedIn or Facebook alumni groups. Reach out to every alumnus in the city where you want to land an interview, find a job, or sell a company, and meet them for coffee or even offer to walk with them from one meeting to another meeting if you have limited resources or if they have limited time. I don't mean text, I don't mean tweet, I don't mean Snap them a picture of you using the dog-ear filter. Meet them in person. Even for fifteen minutes. Putting a name with a face is incredibly useful in a world where we can just as easily skip over an email. This applies whether or not they work in the field that you are interested in. If someone is successful in their career, chances are they have a strong network of their own. If you can make a good impression on them, they might be willing to pass your information along to other people in their network who can help you get the interview that you really want. The larger you can grow your network, the better off you will be—and if you are always thinking about how you need to Network or Die, that will happen faster than you can imagine. The only thing better than having a network of your own is impressing someone with a killer network who will open their network up to you. Overnight your network doubles in size. In the case of your new best alumnus friend, you already have an emotional connection—your alma mater—and who doesn't love sharing stories about their time in high school, college, or business school?

Have family friends who know someone who works in an industry that you are interested in? Reach out to them to ask for an introduction and follow up immediately. The Most Powerful Woman in the Room doesn't waste time being timid, and she shouldn't. Anyone who has hit a certain point in their career is used to being asked this favor, and those of us in the know, we know that it behooves us to take the call/meeting/coffee date. We may find our next assistant, learn something new, or simply feel revitalized by interacting with someone so passionate about our industry that they remind us why we got into it in the first place. Whether the meeting happens or not, always be sure to circle back with the family friend and let them know the outcome. Networking is about constant communication—the more people know where you are in the process, the more they can help you move to the next stage.

When I receive a request from a friend or colleague who is looking for a new job, I almost always recommend that they go through my LinkedIn profile and look for anyone who could be helpful in their pursuit of a career. If I know you and you have made a favorable impression on me, I am more than happy to reach out to someone from my network to connect you to them. I haven't requested a LinkedIn connection in years, and yet I still have thousands of connections because I accept requests from almost anyone. People who are reaching out to connect with me are doing it because they foresee a need that I might be able to service, or they know someone who might know me. If that is the case, there is a strong possibility that I could use their services or wisdom in the future.

So, in this dream scenario, everything has gone well, you have landed your dream job at a company, but you're at entry level.

How do you work your way up?

How do you increase your visibility and gain loyalty that will add to your network?

Use every opportunity that presents itself to meet people, and

110

always say yes when someone invites you to do something that will allow you to meet more people.

As I mentioned earlier, my first internship was all about shredding paper and wiping down the lunch table so that I could use it for other tasks, like packing gift bags. During my second internship, in the events department, I might as well have set up a mattress at work. The busy season in the auction world is nonstop. In the events department at an auction house there are events all day, every day, and every single evening. The three members of the events team divided up the workload equally so they did not have to stay every night for every event.

But let's remember. I was hanging off the very bottom rung of a steep career ladder, and my approach needed to be different and impactful. And even if I wasn't entirely aware of what my career track would be in those early years, I was certain that if I decided to move elsewhere, I would always need good references moving forward.

My strategy? Hustle. And then Network or Die. I made myself an intern who was completely invaluable to the team. I stayed every single night for every single event and acted as a greeter, a table check-in person, an assistant providing directions to guests moving from one area to another; during a couple of events when our guests arrived en masse I jumped into the coat check to help hang coats—anything that would put me in a position where I could spend time with senior colleagues (who finally had a chance to relax over a glass of wine after a long day at the office) or with clients of the company. I memorized names, I memorized faces, and I tried to remember things that they told me or what they were wearing so that I could mention it the next time I saw them. Relationships that started when I was an intern checking people in for dinner at the age of twenty-one turned into a network that I utilized greatly when I was the person hosting the events years later.

If you are reading this book while you are in college and are heading off to do your first internship at a company, remember to be positive and eager no matter what you are asked to do. Even if your internship seems like a total waste of time, the network that you are forming and the relationships that you are making are the building blocks for a lifelong career. Even though you may only be interning for one specific team, your pass to get into the building means that you have the opportunity to meet anyone within that company. And the Most Powerful Woman in the Room is road-mapping her career from the first day of her internship until she ultimately gets what she wants.

But if you have a job and have been in it for a couple of years, how do you continue to grow your network?

Advancing in your career is about knowing people—the right people—and making a good impression. In most companies there are plenty of opportunities for networking internally, so take advantage of any type of social gathering to meet as many of your colleagues as possible. Forming a personal connection with people in the workplace is critical at a time when everyone prefers to email their comments, thoughts, and even criticisms. I always find it amazing to watch how quickly arguments escalate over email when they would never even happen in the first place if people were sitting across from each other. What has saved me time and time again is the advice I give to my team: "Step away from the keyboard, get off your email, pick up the phone and call them, walk over to their desk." If something can't be resolved in a stop by their desk to discuss it, suggest meeting for a cup of coffee or even a glass of wine if you think it might get a little heated. Your internal colleagues are as important to your network as your external relationships, because not only do you want to work in a pleasant environment every day but also, ultimately, some of the colleagues will leave and work for other companies. Should you ever want to work for another company, you had better hope that none of your previous colleagues are in a position where they could give negative feedback during your interview process or before you arrive in a new position. Additionally, if they are moving into a new company and you are on good terms, you suddenly have a new network of people at your fingertips.

And for those people who are talented enough to rise to the top of their company, my advice is to always take an interest in the interns and junior staffers within your company. In many ways, identifying good talent and grooming those people for their next role either internally or externally is the ultimate in networking. Have you ever heard the phrase "rising tides float all boats"? Although this phrase probably wasn't meant to describe building your network underneath you, it certainly works, in my opinion.

In my twenty-year career at Christie's, I have had the opportunity to work with fabulous interns, assistants, and junior staff members. For those who worked hard, made a positive impression because of their willingness to pitch in, and were unafraid of challenges, I am happy to be their advocate as they look for their next step. While you may believe that your network is made up of your peers and people above you in your company, the truth is that the longer you are in the working world, the more important the people you cultivate at the beginning of your career become in time. The women and men who interned for me at Christie's in my early years have become rock stars in their own fields. They work for companies like Goldman Sachs and Fendi, own galleries around the world, or have started their own companies. Because I took the time to get to know them when they worked on my team and have remained in contact with them over these years, it is an easy call whenever I am looking for information in an area in which I am not familiar. I will always take calls, grab coffee, and keep in touch with those people because they extend the network that I have created, and I truly enjoy seeing them succeed. In fact, when I was reaching out to people to contribute advice or stories in the book, I contacted a few of my old interns to ask if they could make introductions to people in their networks.

Earlier this year I received a call from a powerhouse woman in my network who had suggested to her friend who writes for *Forbes* that she interview me for a piece about selling. This is a perfect example of a person in my network who has opened up her network to help me. "Selling Your Vision and Other Advice from One of Christie's Top Auctioneers" was the title of the piece that was published a few weeks after our initial conversation. In my third tip, titled "Network to Finesse Your Story (and Improve Your Odds)," I state, "Networking is the single most important part of selling anything—yourself, your vision, your business." A few weeks later that quote was pulled out of the piece and included on the *Forbes* Instagram account, where it garnered more than 37,000 likes within two days. Clearly I am not the only one who understands the value of a good network! My point in mentioning this is to show you how a network grows the minute you become part of someone else's network. Remember, I didn't know anyone at *Forbes*; a powerful woman with a network of her own knew someone at *Forbes*.

The Most Powerful Woman in the Room knows that growing

her network is paramount to success in life and in business. There is no time like the present. Starting today, I challenge you to begin growing your network. Set a goal that is realistic for you to accomplish: reach out to one new person in the office for lunch or a cup of coffee every two weeks; set up a meeting or a call with someone over LinkedIn once a month to learn more about their journey and tell them about yours; connect with another person on the playground or at school drop-off and set up a time to get together once a semester. Remember that networking isn't about work; it is about getting to know someone on a personal level. The more varied and extensive your network, the easier it will become to sell your ideas and vision. It's all about your *network*. Or as my dad would say, "Network or Die."

building and working their networks

ALEXANDRA LEBENTHAL

Named the "Queen of Wall Street"
by *Fortune* Magazine

Many women don't know where to start networking. To that I say, be a joiner! Whether it is groups within your company, other organizations, or charities, there is no shortage of places to meet people. I would argue that getting involved in charitable organizations is one of the best ways to network. You not only gain exposure to people from many different walks of life, coming together with a shared passion to do good, but you also may have the opportunity to meet some powerful people who sit on the board or have other leadership positions.

A lot of people think that networking is about going to events and meeting people, but it is really about cultivating a group of people who can be instrumental to you, and, equally important, you to them. When I meet someone and we have any kind of meaningful conversation, they go into my physical contacts, but also into my mental Rolodex. I begin a gradual process of getting to know them. If I see good news about someone or their organization, I will send a short email. I also reach out to people when there is news that may not be positive. People appreciate those emails and calls more than the congratulatory ones. Figure out how you can connect people you know with one another in ways that are beneficial to them. Find ways to do that, like having a lunch or dinner for a group of people.

There are some important rules to remember when networking. The second contact you have with someone should not be to ask for something. That is a way to immediately turn someone off. Also, there may be times when someone does not respond to your efforts to connect with them. Don't push it. Just move on to those who will.

ASHLEY MILES

Chief Client Officer, Head of Advertising, Refinery29

Although networking *is* essential to success, I do believe that genuine, meaningful relationships with mutual investment are an important way to grow your career and personal world, all while finding joy in those relationships. On a daily basis, I am in constant contact with the incredible women who've achieved tremendous success before me (past bosses, industry "greats," mentors) to learn from their life "wins" and mistakes. I am also engaged with young people who keep me on the cutting edge of all things cool and important to young women. I spend a lot of time seeking inspiration from creative visionaries and entrepreneurs inside and outside of my industry to diversify my thinking and mind-set. Refinery29's creative talent is medicine to my soul, and collaborating with the world's most influential brands and agencies every day through award-winning activations like 29Rooms and new innovations keeps me constantly inspired, all while expanding my personal and professional network.

TIFFIN JERNSTEDT

Senior Vice President of Communications, PVH Corp.; Founder of Talk Shop

Networking helps you learn about other roles, responsibilities, structures, and companies. When I feel like I'm struggling in my role or company, networking makes me realize that many people have the same challenges, no matter the industry, the company, or their role.

Networking can help reaffirm that you are at the right place, or it can inspire you to keep fighting for the right role or to switch companies to find a role that is a better fit.

I believe networking helps you be a more informed professional and manager. The intel can be invaluable. Listening to how another communications person in a different industry attacks a challenge is an unbelievable learning experience that you can take back to your team and apply within your own company.

And above all else, it is way more *fun* to learn and grow by being social and engaged with people!

THE MOST
POWERFUL
WOMAN
IN THE
ROOM . . .

7

commands her audience

If you really think about it, you have been practicing public speaking from the moment that you opened your mouth and babbled a few words in front of your parents.

The first day of preschool when you raised your chubby, glue-covered fingers to answer the teacher's question, you were speaking in public. When you nervously played the part of a tree with one line in your fourth-grade play, you were practicing public speaking. And don't forget that meandering speech you made after too many glasses of wine at your best friend's wedding. We can count that as public speaking. Even when you speak up in a meeting of four people, you are practicing the art of speaking in public. It shouldn't be a big deal when someone asks you to stand up and make a speech or give a presentation to a room of twelve people. Right?

Tell me if any of this rings true. Someone has asked you to make a speech. You agree because it seems like a good idea . . . and you start thinking about what you are going to say. You write the speech, but the night before, you can't sleep, and then you start to worry that you are going to be too tired to make sense, so you end up tossing and turning the whole night. After feeling exhausted and slightly nauseated all day, the moment arrives and you stand up to make your speech—adrenaline rushes in, you find that your knees and legs feel like Jell-O, and you are clutching your notes like they are the lyrics to a never-released Rihanna song. When you attempt to speak, your voice immediately cracks. All you know is that you have never felt relief like the relief that you feel when you end the speech with "thank you."

I have been taking auctions for around fifteen years—somewhere between 70 and 100 auctions a year. Let's say that, on average, I have been on an actual stage between 1,050 and 1,500 times in my life. The interesting thing about charity auctioneering is that in the nightmare scenario I have described above, at the very least you have the chance to prep for your speech and rehearse it a few times. I can tell you that if you are already nervous about public speaking, charity auctioneering would be your personal hell. When I walk onstage, I usually have a time estimate for how long they want the auction to take (usually around thirty minutes) and a sheet of paper with enough text to fill about two minutes if read without taking a break. So the other twenty-eight minutes is about coming up with enough interesting material to keep the crowd entertained and raise as much money as possible. It's like driving on a perfectly smooth road along the interstate and then veering off onto a road in the Amazonian jungle. I liken it to public speaking while someone is tossing tennis balls at my face.

Once the auction begins, it is inevitable that within the first five minutes an overserved guest will start shouting out his inner monologue or heckling me like we are at a sports arena instead of a black-tie dinner. Within ten minutes, one of the event organizers usually remembers something that she forgot to tell me and starts gesticulating wildly, trying to pantomime something that I am supposed to guess while keeping track of the bidders, their paddle numbers, and my train of thought. By the end of the auction, a waiter has dropped a glass that shattered into a million pieces in front of the stage, someone's phone is ringing loudly, and the puppy that we were supposed to have as a surprise lot decided to run out onstage to the delight of the audience. The first few times I walked onstage, I felt unnerved, never knowing what was about to take place. But after so many years of practice, I find that each audience is like a puzzle without defined borders and it is up to me to figure out how to create a pitch so attractive that the pieces all come together.

Instead of asking you to spend the next fifteen years of your life traipsing across a thousand stages in your quest to ace your next public speaking opportunity, I am going to share some of the key lessons that I have learned over the years to help you rock your next public speaking moment like it has never been rocked before. I want you to be in the bathroom after your speech and overhear, "That was the best speech I have ever heard," or "I laughed, I cried—why doesn't that woman have her own show?" It doesn't matter if it is a presentation for your college class, a last-minute meeting to sell your company to an investor, or a chance to make it right with your best friend after you were too drunk to make one iota of sense during her rehearsal-dinner speech. Being a good public speaker is critical in your journey to be the Most Powerful Woman in the Room.

Twice a year at Christie's, I host tryouts for potential charity auctioneer candidates. The tryouts last three or four days and are open to anyone within the company. The class begins with a group of fifteen to twenty candidates. Ultimately I am looking for the candidates who will represent Christie's at charity auctions around the United States. Similar to what happens on prime-time reality shows like *Survivor* and *The Bachelorette*, I will whittle that number from fifteen to twenty candidates down to three or four people. Happily, you don't have to travel farther than the auction room downstairs or end up engaged to someone you have probably met only nine times. But unlike in those shows, the reward is not a million dollars or a car or a soul mate; it is the chance to get onstage on behalf of Christie's as many times as you can to support charities around the world. The opportunity is open to anyone in the company from a new assistant to the most senior executive. But I will tell you that the people who are the most successful charity auctioneers for Christie's do not attain that status because of their seniority. Instead, they are the ones who take as many auctions as they possibly can—night after night, weekend after weekend, holidays, traveling across the country and in some cases across the world to hone their skill so that no stage seems too large and no audience too small. And while you may not be working for a company that supports a skill like auctioneering, you *can* work public speaking into every day of your life.

But, as with everything in life, it is going to take practice. A lot of practice.

So close your eyes and imagine yourself dressed in your favorite outfit—you know, the one that makes you feel like a million bucks—and join me as I walk into the main saleroom at Christie's Auction House in New York City.

To give you a sense of what it takes to be a charity auctioneer at the world's leading auction house, I want to walk you through the process that I use to identify and train some of the best in the business. Even if you have no intention of moving to New York to work for Christie's, you can use it to ensure that whenever you are speaking in public, you will be the Most Powerful Woman in the Room. By explaining why I make the decisions that I make and why I choose the people that I choose, I hope I can help you gain an understanding of what you should focus on to knock them dead in your next public speaking opportunity.

On the first day of tryouts, all the candidates arrive and sit in our auction chairs as if they are attending one of the sales in our main saleroom. In front of them we have set up a wooden podium with a gavel resting on the top. Roughly twenty seats face the podium, and in the back we have a video camera where I record each candidate as they are trying out. Most of them sit whispering quietly or nervously flipping through a book of auction lots that I have asked them to review in advance of the session. I use the first thirty minutes of class to lay out the ground rules for the tryouts, talk to them about how the charity auctioneer selection process works, and describe what I am looking for when I am selecting charity auctioneers. It all seems very civilized . . .

And then I throw the curveball.

"Now I want everyone to stand up at the podium and tell a story, a joke, or something that they want to share with the class that they can wrap up in two to three minutes. I will give you a few minutes to think about this, and then I am looking for a volunteer to start us off."

Put yourself in their shoes right now. Can you feel your heart start to beat a little faster? Your pulse race? I can still remember when the auctioneering coach said those words at the beginning of my tryout and the feeling of ice water running through my veins as the knot started to build in my stomach.

From my vantage point on the podium, I can tell you what I see when I say those words . . .

Confusion, panic, fear, mainly fear . . . I watch these emotions and more dash across the faces of the candidates as they stare up at me. Try to remember that I have probably worked with every single person whom I am about to judge as part of the tryout process. If we were in the middle of a meeting or walking down the hall, our exchange would be friendly and jovial; in some cases they might have even told me the story that they are about to stand up and tell the class. But for some reason, the thought of having to stand up in front of twenty people they know makes every single person in the room want to sprint out the door and never come back.

Thankfully, most of the time they stay (although I have lost a few over the years at this point in the tryout process).

After I give the class approximately five minutes to think about what they are going to say, I ask for a volunteer. I am 99 percent sure I was the first volunteer in my class, and in nine out of ten cases, the first person to volunteer usually passes the class. This person is a natural-born salesperson for whom sales and speaking are part of their DNA. Quite frankly, the other nineteen people in the class can breathe a sigh of relief because this person has successfully bought them another five minutes to work on their stories. You can hate that person for their natural talent but love them because they are buying you time. After that person has blown everyone away with their incredible story—using humor, eye contact, a relaxed pose, and a killer punch line, we get to the rest of the group. And for me, that is where the fun begins.

The next hour is spent watching each candidate as they tell their story, joke, or whatever comes to mind in the moment, and

assessing whom I can work with over the next three days and ultimately feel comfortable putting onstage for a small charity auction within the month.

As I watch each person tell their story, I take copious notes that
I refer to over the course of that day and the next few days during
tryouts while looking at the following:

1. Can this candidate think on their feet, or do they keep losing their train of thought? Are they able to present the story
   in a way that keeps the attention of the audience?
2. Do they seem comfortable onstage, or do they have a number of nervous tics that are obvious to the audience? When
   they speak do they seem open to the audience. Are they making eye contact or staring straight down at the floor?
3. What kind of story did they choose to present? Did they
   choose something humorous, heartfelt, or sincere? Did they
   use a punch line, or did the story just peter out?

None of these things will eliminate a candidate from the tryouts,
but I need to understand what has to be addressed immediately in
order to figure out how to train each candidate. To address these
issues, I work on each element separately in the days that follow.

Candidates who have been cut after the first day inevitably
come to my office for feedback in the weeks and months that
follow the class. My answer is pretty much always the same. If
public speaking isn't a natural skill, you need to practice it like a
muscle that you work out at the gym. And if you want to be really
good at it, you need to practice it like Gwyneth Paltrow practices
the Tracy Anderson Method. A lot. The more you practice your
skill, the stronger it will become over time. I know many of you

are thinking that you aren't in an office or a place where you can practice in front of a group. I challenge that. You are in front of audiences in all facets of your life. Over the course of this year at my children's school alone, I spent no less than ten nights at parent meetings where I would ask a question or two. At work I am constantly in meetings with large groups of people where I need to make a comment or elaborate on a point. On auction days I find that I am warming up for the stage almost the entire day, practicing banter with people in my office, striking up conversations with strangers in line for lunch, practicing the art of selling to a person in line in front of me to see if I can upsell them on something that is strategically placed on the counter. I practice with a friend or an assistant, a stranger or a person that I have met a couple of times. A lot of times they aren't even aware that I am practicing, but I am testing out jokes or talking about relevant topics of the day that I could use as fodder for the auction that evening. The more you do it, the better you get, and the easier it is to shake off your less-than-best performance. The easiest way to mitigate a lot of the issues that people face in public speaking is preparation. I don't mean reading the speech once in the mirror in your bathroom. I mean talking through your speech over and over again to different people, running it over and over in your head, and then practicing it in every reflective surface you can find. In the auctioneering class, I am throwing people into the deep end to see if they sink or swim. Most of you won't ever be in a similar situation—so breathe a sigh of relief; you will have time to prepare.

The biggest barrier to entry when it comes to public speaking is stage fright or nerves. Let's talk about how to conquer them before you go onstage. As I mentioned before, preparation is the biggest key to ensuring that you are ready for your talk or speech.

It should be so ingrained that nothing can shake it loose, despite your nerves trying to push it out of your brain. One thing I will tell you is that even the most seasoned performer gets nervous in the minutes leading up to the moment when they go onstage. Trust me, I have been backstage with some of the biggest celebrities in the world, and I can see that they are getting the same adrenaline rush that I am getting in the moments before we go on. They start fidgeting like I do, pacing, glancing at their notes like a high schooler cramming for a pop quiz, clicking and unclicking their pen at a rapidly increasing clip.

Typically about five minutes before I go onstage, I begin to feel like I have flown past a cop doing ninety miles an hour in a sixty-mile-an-hour zone. When I first started taking auctions, that feeling made me want to throw up, pass out, or run for the hills. But after all these years onstage, I know the feeling well and have learned that I can use those nerves and that extra energy for my performance. What I want you to do the next time that you can feel the adrenaline coursing into your veins is to recognize it for what it is: a tool to help amp you up and get you ready to rock the crowd in front of you. That adrenaline gives you energy, it helps your mind access the sharpest part of your personality, it makes what could seem like a very dull performance lively if used correctly. So take deep breaths, make sure that your knees are bent, and wiggle your fingers and toes. It isn't giving the speech or taking the auction that is actually scary—it is the anticipation of the speech or the performance that causes the nerves. It doesn't matter how nervous I get before an auction; I always know that the minute my gavel strikes the podium and I launch into my opening line, the nerves will begin to dissipate immediately. Try to remember that whenever you are waiting to get up and present:

the moments before are the worst. Once you start speaking, it will get easier with every second that passes.

One of the most helpful things for me when combating nerves is my Strike. Now that you are aware that your nerves will be on overdrive right before you do any sort of speaking, you can understand the importance of having your Strike ready to go from the first minute you get onstage. There is no better way to conquer this fear than to have your opening sentence memorized. I don't mean sort of memorized. I mean like etched in your brain so that no matter how nervous you are when you get up there, the sentence almost becomes your brain's version of an auto reply. If you are starting out, it can be a question to the audience: "How is everyone doing today?" If you are more advanced, it can be something that shows off your personality or gives insight into who you are going to be as a speaker. When you get up to speak, the audience is staring up at you expectantly—they are open, engaged, ready for whatever you are about to say. If you immediately stare down at your notes, you are cutting yourself off from them before you even start the speech. By memorizing the first line, you can keep your head up and a smile in place, and it will give you a moment to connect with the audience from the minute you start your speech. This also helps calm any nerves that you might feel leading up to the presentation.

One other pro tip that I will throw out there for people who are a little more comfortable with public speaking: toss out your notes. I used to hang on to my notes with the best of them, until a few years ago, when I was catching up with a fellow speaker at a women's conference where I had given a talk titled "The Art of Selling." Initially she praised my speech, but after a few glasses of wine she gave me the advice that has stuck with me ever since:

"You are such a good speaker, but you need to get rid of your notes. No one else knows what you are going to say, so you should try giving speeches without them. You will get a better response from the audience." I had been taking auctions for almost twelve years without a script, but it had never occurred to me that I could give a speech without notes. The next speech, I challenged myself to speak without notes, and she was right; it was completely liberating. I didn't say every single thing I wanted to say, but not being stuck reading a script allowed me to incorporate skills that I learned over many years of charity auctioneering. I could call on someone when I noticed them texting instead of listening, or I could ask a question of the group and spend fifteen seconds bantering with the person who raised their hand. Initially I felt nervous and a little unsteady, but in the end it felt natural and fun.

Throughout the speech or presentation, have a theme that you can go back to time and again—that way, if you lose your train of thought, your mind has an anchor it can come back to as many times as needed. Another great way to ensure that you have an anchor is giving your speech with images or a PowerPoint behind you. Again, don't make the slides text-heavy. You want to use bullet points to show off the points you are going to discuss during your speech; you don't want people reading through the equivalent of a book on a screen behind you while you are trying to engage them. Finally, make sure that you have a great closing line. Even if you do meander throughout the speech or presentation, a great closing line will make it a memorable performance.

While I was writing this book, I was honored for my work raising hundreds of thousands of dollars as the auctioneer for the Friends of Hudson River Park Gala. Martha Stewart was presenting me with the award, given by the Playground Committee, which is a group of women dedicated to ensuring that the Hudson River Park and its playgrounds are well maintained for everyone to use. I had a few themes that I wanted to explore in the speech: how the park is a place of respite and inspiration for New Yorkers living in the concrete jungle, how I have used the park as a resource in ever-changing ways throughout my twenty years in New York, and how the community of women in that room had committed their time and resources to making the park the best that it could possibly be for generations to come. As I mulled over the best way to approach the topic of the speech, I thought about my biggest connection to the park, and my mind always went back to the running path.

The Hudson River Park running path has been my savior, my solace, and a joy in my New York life. Once I anchored the speech with that theme, the speech essentially wrote itself. I thought of the running path and all of the things I had experienced while on that path. I wrote about finding the park in my twenties, fresh out of college, single and lacking friends with whom to make weekend plans, and how I looked forward to each run, as it occupied time during what was otherwise a very lonely day. I moved on to write about how I handed out sandwiches to the rescue workers on 9/11 in the park, which was decimated after the terror attacks, and how it was reborn and rejuvenated as the city slowly recovered from that devastating day. I mentioned how as the years passed I would run with friends on the running path and see families on picnic blankets, how I went on one of my first dates with my husband at the mini-golf course on one of the piers that is part of the park, and how the neighborhood is now the place where I have picnics with my family and friends, like those families I'd seen years ago. It has become my family's backyard. A respite to us from the otherwise bustling city of New York.

On the morning I gave that speech, I did what I always do when I need to focus my thoughts and come up with a solution: I went on a run. As I ran, I said the words out loud, remembering each marker on the running path and how it correlated to my life. When I spoke after being introduced by Martha Stewart (that was not intimidating at all, I promise), I imagined myself back on the path so that anytime I felt myself start to drift, I would think about the route and mentally chart the trajectory of my life in New York along that running path. After finishing the part of my speech about the park, I moved on to talk about the incredible difference that a group of women banding together had made in our neighborhood and how proud I was to call downtown Manhattan my home. My final line was thanking my husband and mentioning how I would never want to be on a playground without him and our three kids . . . but as I was finishing up the emotional part of the speech, I couldn't resist adding in a little humor: ". . . and Martha Stewart can come too." I'd spent months working on that speech in my head and delivered it all without notes, but I also practiced it in the mirror, to my ten-month-old, while I was running, in the shower, to my best friend, Mary. Practice makes perfect? Absolutely.

At this point, my hope is that you are thinking about how these tools are going to help you from running away in a panic at your next public speaking opportunity. If nothing else, you can start to think about creating a path for your speech that keeps you on track. So now that we actually have you in a moment when you are presenting, let's talk about your physical presence. If I were hosting tryouts, at this point I would be attempting to figure out what nervous tics the candidates have when they are speaking. In most cases, it is obvious to everyone in the audience almost immediately what the person does when they are nervous; however, the person onstage usually doesn't even realize they are doing it until you point it out.

A nervous tic can be something as simple as saying "um . . . um . . . um" every couple of seconds while you are speaking, or wringing your hands like Lady Macbeth trying to remove that damned spot. Or it can be that your voice quiets to a whisper or ends up so high in pitch that windows might be breaking in a nearby room. My nervous tic on my first day of tryouts was flipping my long hair back and forth, back and forth, whenever I was auctioning off a lot. The auctioneering coach broke the habit by interrupting with a "put your hand down" every time I would start to flip it while I was at the podium. I wore my hair up for the next three days of tryouts just so I wasn't tempted to flip it. Once you point out a nervous tic, people often get a little distracted trying to fix it, but they can usually get rid of it within a day or two. The same goes for changing their voice pitch and volume. One of my candidates tried out a couple of years ago and her voice would go from totally normal to incredibly high and squeaky every time she started to sell a lot. I tried to explain the difference, but she couldn't hear it until we videotaped her performance. Halfway through the videotape, she squealed with laughter and said, "Dear god, turn it off—I can't take it for one more second." Truthfully, we all felt the same way. An easy technique to figure out your nervous tics is to read a speech in front of a friend or two and use your phone to record it. You will be amazed at the things you do when you are nervous that you don't even notice until you watch yourself on camera. Moreover, once you realize how to correct the issue, your audience will have a much better time watching you because they won't be distracted by your hair flipping or leg shaking, or using their fingers to plug their ears against your high voice.

The final piece that I watch closely as the candidates speak is what kind of story they choose to tell. It is often the most important part of the tryout because it quickly shows what will be critical to their speaking success. When I tried out, I told a childhood story that has been repeated throughout my life whenever I am finding something particularly challenging or difficult. The way my parents tell the story . . . they dropped me off at ski school at the age of five, along with two of my other siblings, and headed up on the chairlift for their first run. A couple of runs in, they were on the chairlift and saw a note on the dry-erase board at the top of the mountain asking them to return to the ski school to pick me up. Fearful that something had happened, they rushed back to the school, only to find me sitting in a corner, refusing to ski and eating snow by the handful. When my mother asked me what was wrong, I stared up at her pitifully and told her that all they wanted me to do was "work, work, work." Incidentally, my husband jokingly says, "Work, work, work" whenever I am complaining about something. It still makes me laugh out loud when I hear it.

Sharing that story is very much who I am—my life is an open book—and my stories are shared with strangers as often as they are shared with close friends. My story is indicative of who I am as a speaker and an auctioneer—there is always a personal anecdote to go along with whatever I am doing onstage. I think that a well-delivered story is one where the arc leads you right into a punch line that will keep you laughing for days. In most cases, the story that the candidates choose to tell helps show me which personality tools they will use most effectively onstage. If their story is humorous, there is a good chance that humor will be something I can help them develop to use to their advantage while onstage. If they choose a story that is particularly touching or sincere, it is probably humanity and earnestness that will endear them to an audience. Any and all of these qualities are effective, and the most talented speakers use them all together to deliver a knockout speech every time.

The way they wrap up a speech is also important. Did it end with a witty joke that summed up the story or did it go out with a whisper? I take these things into account as I narrow the field on who my final candidates will be over the following days. As you assess what will be your strength as a speaker, think about what kind of story you would tell if you had five minutes to prepare. Humorous? Empathetic? A life experience of someone else that you observed?

At the beginning of the auction process, each candidate receives an auction book filled with lots that one of our auctioneers has sold over the years. Each candidate is asked to spend time preparing for the sale of the lots and selling them. Once I have figured out which speaking style works for the candidate, I challenge them to lean on that quality each time they are onstage. Since we are raising money for nonprofits, people who have an earnest, empathetic side can use that to relate to the audience. If humor is their weapon of choice, I ask them to pick the most effective times to use it. Even with the most riveting speaker, there will be times when everyone in the audience is starting to look a little glassy-eyed. When planning your speech, a well-placed joke threaded throughout the speech engages and reengages the audience. If humor is not your thing, an emotional connection can be just as effective if placed strategically throughout a speech or presentation.

Once you have had a chance to practice everything that we have discussed thus far, it is time to understand the most crucial part of selling: how to sell to your audience. It doesn't matter if you are speaking to a group of ten people in a senior citizens' home or onstage with Tony Robbins. The following things are mandatory if you want to be remembered for your performance.

1. You bring the energy you want from your audience.

Enthusiasm is infectious. Enthusiasm in public speaking is CRITICAL.

Most nights that I take auctions, I am in the unenviable position of going onstage after everyone has been sitting at dinner for over two hours. You can see it in people's eyes as they start to check their watches and remember that it is a weeknight. The heavy entrée sitting in their stomach is making them feel sober and tired, and the nonstop speeches that seemed interesting are now starting to sound a little dull. By the time I get onstage, two-thirds of the room is staring at me with a dead-behind-the-eyes look. If I walk out with anything less than a huge smile, a commanding presence, and a solid gavel strike, it is immediately reflected in the faces of the audience.

I bring the energy that I want from the room—and let me tell you, they know it from the minute I hit the stage. Even during the auction, as attention starts to wane after a few lots, I am constantly challenging the audience to stay with me by keeping my energy level high and my performance on point. Humor is my tool, and any time I feel the energy in the room getting low, I throw in a joke. You can easily do the same thing the next time you are giving a presentation. If you see someone yawn in the audience, a quick "Sir, I saw that yawn—I will try to be a little more entertaining to keep you engaged," said with a big smile, works every time. Likability as a presenter is a winning strategy.

Another question I'm always asked when I get offstage is "How do you psych yourself up after a long day spent getting your kids up and to school and a full day at the office, followed by getting your kids into bed and heading back out to take an auction at night?" I started taking auctions when I was twenty-four years old, so you can imagine that in my fifteen-year career as an auctioneer, I have had nights when I was tired, sick, and even a little hungover. When I entered my thirties and had three children in four and a half years, I hit a level of exhaustion and sickness I did not even know existed. Did I mention I took auctions until I was nine months pregnant with each of my kids? There were times when I would get into a cab on the way to the auction and literally fall asleep between the cab leaving my apartment and arriving at the event venue. Typically I use a variety of different tools to keep myself alert and focused on the evening ahead; I try to find time for some type of exercise on auction days, whether that be a run (I never take a business trip without my running shoes to shake off the flight with a pre-auction run), a ride on a Citi Bike, or even getting off the subway two stops early on the way home so that I can get some fresh air and clear my head. If that isn't an option, I will put on my headphones and blast a catchy tune that immediately elevates my mood and my adrenaline level (favorites include anything Top 40 as well as anything that makes me want to dance) as I am heading to the venue. Worst-case scenario, coffee. Good for the performance, not so good for sleep after the performance.

But sometimes it isn't music or exercise; it is simply remembering why I am there that provides the motivation I need. When I was in my early twenties, I arrived at an event only to find out that they had reordered the evening and the auction would be almost an hour later than originally scheduled. As the evening continued, it became apparent that nothing was going as scheduled and that the auction was going to be almost two hours later than we had originally discussed. I was seated next to the development director during the dinner, and as we finally moved closer to the time of the auction, he mentioned something about the operating budget of the organization. Truthfully, I was only half paying attention, as my nerves were starting to set in, and I asked, "What is your operating budget?" He gave a wry smile and said, "You are about to tell me." Talk about a gut check—the entire operating budget for this nonprofit was dependent on what I could coax out of the crowd that evening. I have never forgotten that conversation, and at every opportunity I relay it to people trying out in the auctioneering class. My job onstage on any night is to get every single dollar out of the pocket of someone who can afford it and give it to someone who needs it. In that case, it was the difference between kids getting after-school programming in an at-risk neighborhood, but this motivates me to dig deep no matter how tired I am when I am going onstage. I never forget to use every ounce of energy I have left in my reserves to engage the audience during public speaking. There is nothing to be gained from leaving anything on the table—in a charity auction or in life. So give it your all. Every time.

The next time you are listening to someone you think is a talented speaker, whether a teacher, a professional speaker, or a colleague, take note of what you like about their presenting style. Are they open, present, and enthusiastic about their subject matter? If you find that you are engaged, interested, and enjoying yourself, I would bet a Picasso that they are bringing their energy to the room, and you are benefiting from their enthusiasm.

2. The audience wants you to succeed.

Over the course of my auctioneering career, I have attended more than a thousand benefits in New York City. And while I have been onstage at each of these events, I have also had the pleasure of watching thousands of other people give speeches before I get onstage. You can always tell if someone is a seasoned public speaker by the way they react when something goes wrong during their speech. If someone is uncomfortable when they first get up onstage, it becomes positively painful when something unexpected happens midway through their speech. Take, for instance, the time that a teleprompter had the wrong speech loaded and an honoree stood there repeating, "Something's wrong with the teleprompter," over and over and over again until one of the audiovisual guys came to collect her from the stage. Then there was the time an honoree went up to receive his award and the celebrity presenter, who shall remain nameless, had had so much to drink that he spent fifteen minutes rambling on about personal issues he had with the charity instead of handing over the mike to the honoree. Now, you, because you are training to be the Most Powerful Woman in the Room, would have mentioned the teleprompter once, given a big smile, ad-libbed a few sentences of thanks to the organization, and walked offstage. And the rambling celebrity? You would have seized the moment to put your arm around him, gently take the microphone, and make a kind comment about him before shepherding him off the stage. But the majority of people would never think about anything except for hiding in the wings, because they find public speaking to be the worst thing that they can think of.

What everyone seems to forget as soon as they stand up to give a presentation or a speech is that the people in the audience are human. The audience is rooting for you to make it through your speech because they feel as uncomfortable when you are stuttering and stumbling through it as you do. Instead of looking at a crowd of people through a lens of fear, look at them as a group of people rooting for you. Like your own personal cheerleading squad.

I was attending an auction for GLAAD in San Francisco when a well-known songwriter got up to sing a song that had been at the top of the Top 40 chart for months. When she sang the first verse of the song, I honestly thought that the microphone was broken; her voice was cracking, words were missing, and truthfully it sounded like a total disaster. During the refrain between the first and second verse, she said pitifully to the audience, "I'm sorry, guys—I have crippling stage fright." Did the audience stand up and boo her or throw things at her to get her off the stage? OF COURSE NOT. A fellow songwriter jumped onstage to put his arm around her and help her sing the song.

Soon the entire audience was on its feet and singing along in an effort to show support as she limped through to the end of the song. Did it sound good? No. It sounded absolutely terrible. But the audience went wild when she finished to show that they were on her side; she had overcome her fear and persevered. People understand that public speaking is tough, and they sympathize when it is going badly. If you are a nervous speaker, do not hesitate to message that to the crowd so they understand that this is a struggle for you. People love an underdog, especially an underdog who asks for help.

I took an auction earlier this year when I walked onstage, forcefully banged down my gavel, and spoke directly into the microphone to announce myself . . . only to find that the microphone didn't work. Not like it was cutting in and out; it didn't work at all. Onstage in front of 350 people with a nonworking mike. Not an ideal scenario.

Instead of hitting the eject button from the stage (they don't have one, but there have been nights when I certainly could have used it), I moved in front of the podium so that I was closer to the audience and announced that I was glad the microphone didn't work because now they would have to feel terrible for me if they were talking over me. I smiled while explaining that there was no alternative, that they had to be completely quiet until the audiovisual team brought up a working mike. The audience complied, and halfway through the auction a member of the audiovisual team came running up to hand me a working mike. When my voice went from a loud yell to a voice projected by the power of a microphone, the audience cheered. They didn't want me up there without a microphone any more than I wanted to be up there without one. By turning them into allies, they felt invested in the performance. When I had the tools that I needed to make sure I could succeed, they were there to support me.

3. Make the audience part of your performance.

When I was ten years old, my parents took us to see Jay Leno, who used to host *The Tonight Show* . . . most of you will probably know this as *The Tonight Show with Jimmy Fallon*. But when I was little, Jay Leno was the Jimmy Fallon of late night, and the fact that he was coming to a small town in Louisiana to do a show was a pretty big deal. The show was at the civic center, which was a large stadium where any big musical acts or conferences would take place in town. I sat next to my father, who, before a diagnosis of sleep apnea, spent the bulk of my childhood falling asleep anywhere that he was seated when the lights dimmed—movie theaters, church, concert halls, my college interview . . . no opportunity was missed for a quick catnap. But during that comedy show, I noticed something that stuck with me for years. Midway through the set, Jay Leno started involving people from the audience in his performance— calling out questions like, "What do you do, sir?" and then making up a lighthearted joke as he went along. The crowd was roaring with laughter, and my dad, who had been asleep for most of the act, was suddenly engaged. I noticed that he straightened up in his chair, sitting as tall and erect as he possibly could—almost willing Jay Leno to call on him and ask him a question. To make him the star of that room for a night. It was such a marked difference to the earlier part of the show that, even at my young age, I could clearly see that something about potentially being called on in front of a group of his peers had made him puff up like a penguin.

As I mentioned earlier, I use this trick whether I am speaking to a class of fifteen master's students at Christie's or in front of a crowd of five thousand at Madison Square Garden. Anytime it seems like you are losing people during a speech or presentation, mention something about someone in the crowd and watch how quickly it reengages everyone. Some will be sitting up in their seats trying to catch your eye, while others will be slinking down in their seats trying to avoid eye contact. Either way, they will be paying attention for the next few minutes. Also, don't be rattled by unexpected things that take place during the event. Instead, try to incorporate mundane moments into your speech and watch people's attention pique. If a cell phone rings mid-speech, instead of letting it rattle you, smile at the cell phone offender and say, "Be sure to tell them that I say hi." Speaking to your crowd humanizes *you* as the speaker and makes everyone feel like they are part of the performance. It makes the audience feel like you are talking *to* them (as opposed to talking *at* them), which is what will move you from a good speaker to a great speaker.

When giving any type of presentation, try to speak to the audience as if you are speaking to a group of your friends. Instead of acting like there is a wall between you and the people you are addressing, involve them in your speaking and make them feel invested in the performance.

4. Never underestimate the power of flattery.

A friend and frequent bidder at an auction once confided after a couple of glasses of wine that she used to attend auctions where another auctioneer would use the paddle-raise portion of the evening as his own personal vendetta against the wealthiest guys in the room. As he started calling out numbers at the top level of the paddle raise, he would sandwich it with, "Steve, the *New York Times* told us how much you made last year. You are only going to give that much?" Think of how Steve felt in that moment, immediately embarrassed, a little annoyed when he raised his hand— what he probably wanted to do was raise his middle finger. My friend told me that watching those interchanges kept her from ever raising her paddle at a paddle raise when that auctioneer was at the helm for fear of being called out and embarrassed in front of her peers.

The first time she saw me take an auction, I mentioned the stunning dress that the woman in front of her was wearing when she raised her paddle. The difference? I have a particularly good vantage point from stage for spotting great dresses, and so I always mention it when I take bids: "And the final bid comes from the lady wearing the fabulous red dress—not only generous, but also doing an amazing job of parenting four small children." I'm sure you don't have to guess who can be counted on to raise her hand every time. Negativity in selling is a waste. You end up alienating people, insulting people, and turning people off. Keep it positive, keep it light, and make people feel the best that you possibly can whenever you are the person commanding the room.

The Most Powerful Woman in the Room knows the importance of selling her vision to those around her. Public speaking is a critical tool for ensuring that you are ready to make yourself heard. There is no question that it is going to take a lot of "work, work, work," but the more you practice, the more prepared you will be the next time that someone needs you to give a last-minute talk to a group. Grab your phone, get in front of the mirror, and start practicing!

public speaking

JULIA TAYLOR CHEEK

**Founder & CEO, EverlyWell; landed one of
the largest deals in *Shark Tank* history**

When preparing for a presentation, think about what the audience wants to learn. So much of a good presentation is the audience thinking they learned something, or that they were entertained.

For TechCrunch's Startup Battlefield, I had six minutes onstage to pitch EverlyWell and go through a live product demo for thousands of people in the audience and 30,000 people watching online. This was not a presentation to fly by the seat of your pants. To be sure I could deliver, I flew out to San Francisco two days early and practiced the presentation over and over again while recording it on my iPhone. You have to rehearse the speech enough times that it becomes natural—much like how professional athletes practice, watch tape, and adjust. I was up first, and I delivered confidently, even over the noise of the construction crew setting up and the twenty other entrepreneurs I was competing against.

I was convinced after TechCrunch that I could handle any public speaking engagement, until *Shark Tank* came along. *Shark Tank* is a great example of how important Q&As are in a presentation. While the prepared pitch is only ninety seconds, you have to be ready to think on your feet and overcome your nerves—and know that anything you say can be used for national TV. Often when you watch presentations with Q&As, you'll notice that speakers present and then become very casual with the question-and-answer portion. This is an opportunity to shine and reiterate your key points.

Speaking is simply storytelling, and it will become natural with practice and opportunity. Make your key points in your own speaking style, and learn to speak naturally. Some of the tips and tricks like "power posing" may not work for you, which is *why just doing it* is the best way to learn your own style. Eventually, you can be your authentic self and feel like you are just talking to your group of friends, telling a story about your weekend.

ALEXANDRA WILKIS WILSON

Cofounder, Gilt Groupe and GlamSquad;
SVP of Consumer Strategy and Innovation, Allergan

When it comes to public speaking, I like to throw out a question or two to warm up the room and also get a sense of the audience: "How many of you are currently an entrepreneur or think one day you may start a company of your own?"

Back in my Gilt days, I would always say, "Raise your hand if you are a member of Gilt."

I really try to emotionally connect with my audience, and I always smile. If it is a small meeting or pitch, I do research on the people in advance and try to find some common ground to mention as an icebreaker.

If I see via LinkedIn that a person I am meeting has a friend in common with me, I will first check with my friend to make sure the relationship is in good standing, and then I might mention this to casually break the ice. I also typically do a quick one-minute check to see if the person is active on social media so I can be familiar with their content and can potentially refer to something posted. I don't advocate coming off like a stalker when breaking the ice, but rather as someone who does their homework! If I am meeting with representatives from a brand, I study the company online and/or in retail in advance so that I am current on their newest product lines and company news.

THE MOST
POWERFUL
WOMAN
IN THE
ROOM...

8

creates a road map
and follows through

When the *New York Times* published "Keeping Up With Lydia Wickliffe Fenet," a piece that chronicled a day in my life in October 2017, I expected comments and good natured jokes from my friends and siblings about being featured in such a prominent way. What I did not expect was the comment that seemed to be the main takeaway for most people who read the article: "Wow. You are seriously busy."

You have heard the saying "If you want to get something done, give it to a busy person." I am that person. "How do you do it all?" is something that I hear at least once a week. "All" meaning three kids under five, a job during the day at Christie's, another job as a charity auctioneer at night, and writing this book in my spare time. Of course, not forgetting the most important parts of this entire equation—making quality time for my family, maintaining friendships . . . and trying to make it look totally effortless on Instagram with a catchy caption to attract followers. Because if it doesn't look good on Instagram, did it really happen? I so badly want to say no, but the reality is that I want it to look easy. Sometimes it is, sometimes it isn't. Most often it is somewhere in between.

Take it from someone who has no sense of direction: what you really need is a road map. Sure, Waze is great, but in life you need to sit down and come up with your own plan, one that no algorithm can figure out for you. A step-by-step plan to help you attain your goal and then knock it out of the park. I'll let you in on a secret. For many years my road map had "sell a book" written halfway down the path. Recently I added "sell *at least* a million books" directly below it—and thanks for your help, by the way—because I don't just want to focus on selling a few books. I want to sell books faster than Simon & Schuster can print them. Selling the book was the first step to a larger plan I have for my life. And to set those goals and execute them, I need to maximize my time while still looking forward toward the next opportunity. But this book is about you, so we need to figure out how to get your road map planned out so you can stop looking down and start looking forward.

The most important thing to remember is that creating a road map is not meant to add an additional layer of stress to your busy life; it is meant to help you find more time to focus on the things you want to do. By sitting down and spending just a little time focusing on creating a plan that helps you map out your day/week/month/year, you don't waste time that could be spent achieving your goals.

Time is precious, and to ensure I do not squander one minute, I spend time at the beginning of each week making sure I have a road map in place. In short, from the time I wake up in the morning to the time my head hits the pillow at night, I look at how to structure my day so that I get everything done. It may sound rigid, but in fact, once I have the day laid out in my head (or on a piece of paper nearby), there is plenty of flexibility as things come up. While the plan is set, it can also be changed, but at the end of the day I want to have accomplished everything I set out to do. I watch so many people—friends and colleagues alike—who constantly bemoan the fact that they never have time to do what they want. If they were to sit down and commit to creating a plan for each day, they would find that a lot of the dead time (commuting, driving from point A to B, kids' naptimes, time after you finish work or, if you are a parent, after your kids go to bed) could be used to add minutes or even hours to ultimately help them reach their goals.

If you are reading this chapter in disbelief that someone would put this much thought into creating a structure for her life, I hope it will make you feel better to know that I didn't start out this way. Although I always knew it was important to set goals and follow through on attaining those goals in high school and college, I didn't really think about putting a road map in place to them. After graduating from college and moving to New York with my internship at Christie's secured, I was simply moving through life. Even professionally, much of my success in the early years was due to hard work and being in the right place at the right time when those above me moved on. In conversations that I have with male friends who are my age, many tell of a formative moment when one of their parents sat them down and explained that they needed to study hard and get good grades so that when they were older, they could earn a living and support their family. However, very few of my female friends ever had this type of conversation with anyone. The advice was more like "You can do whatever you want," but there was no expectation or bar that was added to make them sit down and figure out how to get there. But the more I advanced in my career, the more I understood the importance of creating a map to move forward in my career and life. Otherwise it is easy to get stuck in the everyday grind. Look up, take note, and plan for what you want to be ahead of you. If you are working toward something, anything, it will help motivate you to keep up the momentum for everything else in your life. I also find that after I create the road map for what I want to achieve, telling my closest friends about my goals helps to hold me accountable. My friend Mary Giuliani is the person with whom I share all my goals, and vice versa. She is the Gayle to my Oprah, and I am the Gayle to her Oprah. The beauty of our friendship is that we both think that we are Oprah and are so proud of our friend Gayle. Whenever I need someone to remind me of a goal that I set or give me encouragement, I call her. And she knows that I am here to do the same thing for her.

I am sure you are wondering what any of this has to do with selling. This is just time management, right? To me, being prepared in your life—spending time recognizing and setting up your priorities, looking forward at your calendar for the days and weeks ahead, and setting out a long-term road map—is crucial to feeling confident and laser-focused on what you want to achieve.

So let's begin by jump-starting your week. To do that, you need to plan your week before it even starts. I have heard my friends refer to Sunday evening as the Sunday night scaries; it's when a week of work/school/looking for a job/fill in the blank looms ahead. If that is the way you feel, let me help you see it differently. Sunday evening is the time I use to get prepared and excited for the week ahead. In order to do this, I pull out the organizational tool that has been with me through thick and thin. I know you are wondering what app I have found or what piece of technology has helped me organize my life, but in truth I use a paper calendar, which I have printed out from printable[fill in the year]calendars.com for as long as I can remember. (I am sure every person working in tech just died a little on the inside.) A single page displays an entire month with the date in the top right and a box below it filled with nothing but blue sky and opportunity. Don't get me wrong—I have the information on my phone as well, but something about seeing everything mapped out in front of me on paper makes me feel like I have oversight into what the upcoming week and future weeks will bring. In each of the empty boxes, I list work activities, extracurricular activities, kids' activities, family activities, and travel. This helps me prepare for what is coming up and also helps me think through what arrangements I will need to make for everything to run smoothly.

If I have auctions during the week, I set aside time on Sunday for my husband and me to discuss his schedule. We troubleshoot potential scheduling issues: Can he can make it home from work in time for me to head back out for an auction on Tuesday? Do we need to get a sitter to bridge the gap if he can't be there on time? Spending ten minutes setting up the rest of the week also helps me figure out a key ingredient: my wardrobe. Do I need to drop things off at the dry cleaner on the way to drop off the kids at school? Call my friend and get the dress that I loaned her back in time for an auction? Rent something from Rent the Runway or Armarium? Buy something quickly from Net-a-Porter or Moda Operandi?

Knowing that I won't have to scramble to figure out what to wear or realize that I don't have the right dress for a meeting, speech, or auction is a huge relief—and it takes only a little pre-planning to figure it out. Although I fully recognize that very few people need to worry about getting a dress dry-cleaned for an auction, I suspect that more than one of you has stood in front of your closet trying to figure out what to put on for the day while the minutes tick by. Before you know it, you are late, and if you have kids, they are late; and moreover, you are on the back foot from the minute you walk out the door. Get rid of your Sunday night anxiety by being proactive about your life and your schedule.

If you are looking at your weekly schedule with dread, try to incorporate something to look forward to over the course of the week. Take a walk or run with a friend. Meet up after work or school for a picnic playdate with friends. Do not fall into the trap of sitting mindlessly in front of the TV for four hours after you get home from work or finally get the kids into bed. People like to say that there aren't enough hours in the day, but I always wonder how they are using the hours that they have. Set a goal, even a small one, and use the evening hours productively instead of squandering them. If you love a particular show and are prone to binge-watching, try to watch one or two episodes instead of five or six episodes in a row. I wrote the majority of this book in the evenings after putting my kids to bed. My reward was watching an episode of *The Crown* with my husband after I finished a chapter. It kept me motivated to finish and also kept me from squandering time glued to my phone.

What exactly do I mean by a "road map"? Mine range from road maps for busy days to a road map for the next ten years of my life. But the next ten years of life probably seems a little overwhelming, so let's just start with a day when I have three kids (every day!) and a full workday in the office, followed by an auction later that evening.

If it is an insanely busy day, I will write the entire schedule down. If it is a less structured day, I have mental parameters around time that will help guide me through the day. By having a road map for the day in place from the minute I wake up in the morning, I never feel like I spend additional time thinking or worrying about where I need to be or when I need to be there.

But life, as you know, is never as easy as I just made it sound. Whether it's your outfit getting ruined on your commute, traffic delays, or an urgent call from a friend who needs counseling, there are many incidents that can easily blindside an entire morning. Add three young children into the mix and the best-laid plans are always thrown off by the unexpected. At least once a week, I drop my daughter off, only to realize I still have her lunchbox as I head into the subway four blocks away. I have yet to make it all the way to work with Beatrice's monogrammed lunchbox, but it is only a matter of time. The key is to give yourself enough time to allow for those issues by setting yourself up for success in the first place, and the best way to do that is to road-map your day/week/month.

So here we are, average Monday in my life. If you looked on my iPhone you would see the approximate time for each activity on the left and a short description of what needs to take place during that time. In the road map below I have also included a few of my surefire time hacks that can help you own every minute of your day.

6:30 a.m. I tend to wake up naturally around this time and enjoy a few minutes in the morning to myself before the kids get up. I look through emails that came in from Asia overnight and ensure there is nothing urgent that needs a response. I always try to get in a little exercise first thing in the morning, so even if I don't get up early enough to make it out for a long run or a trip to the gym, I will do a few reps of push-ups, sit-ups, and some yoga stretches that are very basic and not at all impressive (but hey, at least I am trying). I truly believe that to have a strong mind you need a strong body. My personal rule that I have followed religiously since high school is never take more than two days off from exercising, because the more time you take off, the more daunting it seems. Even if you aren't feeling motivated, you MUST do it. Early morning, early evening, middle of the day, late at night. Yes, there will be days when you will be tired. Yes, there will be days when you don't want to do anything. Just try to remember: no more than two days off. Even if I can't make it out the door for my favorite type of exercise—running—I use a Citi Bike to get to work on busy weeks. Sure I arrive windswept and always thankful that I have made it alive (New York's Citi Bike is no joke), but I am exercising during a time that I could be sitting on the subway. If you have kids, make their playtime your playtime. They are running around playing soccer? Be the referee and do sprints alongside them. Or use an app to do a little at-home exercise after you put them to bed. No matter how busy your day, there is always time when exercise can be incorporated—looking at a map of your day will help you figure out that timing so that you can build it in.

7:00 a.m. The kids usually wake up around this time. Enter the routine of parents everywhere—wake/feed/cuddle/brush teeth/pack lunch/dress, all while trying to make sure that our little one doesn't dump water on the floor/climb up something/fall off something. Did I mention that I also have to put on makeup, and maybe, MAYBE, curl my hair? Then and only then do I realize that only one of the kids has put on clothes, the other one has food all over his shirt, and we are supposed to be walking out of the door in two minutes. BREATHE.

7:45 a.m. Two parents, two different school drop-off locations. On this morning I leave with our older daughter, who has an 8:15 a.m. start time. If you are like me, your morning doesn't really begin until you have a little caffeine. Mine comes in the form of a latte from Starbucks, ordered in advance by app (it saves me ten minutes). I have it in my hand as we descend into the subway to get to school. Chris, my husband, stays with the younger two children, as our middle son doesn't have to get to school until 8:45 a.m.

8:30 a.m. On the home front our nanny, Rhea, arrives. Chris walks our son to school. If you were viewing this on a split screen, you would hear the bell ringing at our older daughter's school, indicating that it is time to drop off. Big kiss, bigger hug. Off she goes, and Mom goes into overdrive to gear up for the next part of the day.

8:45 a.m. The minute I leave Beatrice to walk to the subway, I transition into work mode. I like to think I have mastered the art of walking and texting, though I am sure that anyone on the side-walk would disagree. I use any spare commuting time to answer emails and check my calendar to make sure I am prepared for all of my meetings that day. I never squander the subway time because it is the only time during the day that people can't reach me. If I drove to work, this is the time I would use to start call-backs if I were alone in a car with any time to spare.

9:00 a.m. I arrive at Christie's and start the seated-at-my-desk part of the day. I say this because if you look back at my morning, I have already spent a solid forty-five minutes working between the earlier part of the day and my subway commute. Sometimes when I arrive at my desk, I just sit and take a few deep breaths. Attending to my kids in the morning starts everything off with such a bang that I need a minute to just be. Once I am feeling a little more centered I log in to my computer to get up to speed. One of my favorite motivational tips came from my best friend Corinne, who changes her work password to reflect her current goal in life. If she is working on a project she needs to complete, her password is the name of the project. If she wants to remind herself to stick with her gym schedule, her password is GET IN SHAPE. Think about how many times a day you type in your password. It is a daily reminder to set goals and follow through. My email password right now is FINISH BOOK#1!

The first fifteen minutes of my work day are spent getting organized. I try to clear my inbox of any emails that have been left over from previous days; I make a list of MUST DO TODAY action items that I put at the top of a notebook that comes everywhere with me; and finally I double-check that I don't have any outstanding school items/doctor appointments/personal admin that needs to get done before everyone arrives around 9:30 a.m.

9:30 a.m. This is always my favorite time of day to hold meetings, as people seem fresh and ready for the day. In many ways it reminds me of the crowd at the beginning of an auction. I find that people are engaged in the morning, alert from their first coffee and more focused and energetic. I was never a morning person until I had kids, but now I find that I love the mornings and I get caught up in the energy from everyone around me.

If you aren't the kind of person who is good at sticking to meeting times, try printing out a calendar of your day and keep it with you at all times. Having a printed calendar keeps my timing front of mind so I can constantly refer to it. I always block off at least thirty minutes at my desk during the day; otherwise I leave the office feeling like I am totally behind in all the work I need to do but up to speed on what everyone else wants me to know.

12:00 p.m. As I have mentioned many times before, I like meeting face-to-face. If I am meeting a new prospective client, I often ask them to lunch in order to get to know them better than I would over a cup of coffee or a phone call. If I am not meeting someone, it is a quick round-trip to the nearest lunch spot to pick up lunch and get back to my desk. A work hack I love to pass along to anyone who complains about not being able to get to their boss for answers is to use "travel times"—to walk that person to/from meetings or even to pick up lunch with them. One member of my team does this regularly on days when she knows I am in back-to-back meetings all day. That fifteen minutes would have been tacked onto the end of my day if we hadn't spent that time together—by the time I get back to my desk, she has everything she needs and I am able to carry on with my day. Another colleague offered to do the same thing when I was walking to a lunch meeting a few blocks away. He was scheduled, I was scheduled, and the only time we found open was my five-block walk—so he walked with me to my lunch meeting, we talked strategy, and he picked up his lunch on the way back. Not every day will be that busy, but if you have a lot to do, remember there is dead time in your schedule that can be used as well.

2:00 p.m. My afternoons are usually spent returning phone messages, meeting with potential partners, talking to auction committees about ways to raise more money at their event, or brainstorming new partnership strategies with my team. I have noticed that the later in the day it gets, the more coworkers come by for leisurely office chat. The truth is, you will spend more time with your coworkers than with almost anyone else in your life aside from your immediate family. Do you see your best friends five days a week for eight to twelve hours a day at a stretch? The friendships and the bonds that you form with your coworkers can help enhance your work experience while also expanding your network. Yes, they are colleagues, but if you support and help one another along the way, there is no reason that you can't be friends outside the office as well. One of my closest friends worked on my events team. When I say "closest," I mean closest. I was a bridesmaid in her wedding and she was a bridesmaid in my wedding.

People often express disbelief that I have been in the same place for twenty years. However, I have been able to stay and succeed because I have good relationships with my colleagues, I care about their well-being, and I try to keep relationships positive whenever possible. And while relationships with your colleagues are an important part of life, also know that there are colleagues who can be a complete black hole of time in your day when you are racing to get home or to another job or a workout class. Don't get me wrong—I enjoy long conversations with friends and colleagues as much as the next woman. But these days I am working against a hard stop to get home, especially on auction days. After so many years at the same company, I am very aware of my colleagues, who can easily take away an hour of my day when they "drop by" to tell me something. I learned years ago that in order to maintain good relationships with chatty people, a quick five-minute drop-by to their cubicle or office once a week is all it takes to show interest without giving up control of your day clock. Instead of feeling like you are constantly at the mercy of someone else who is pushing your end time later and later in the day, you can wrap up the conversation or leave whenever you feel like you need to without having to ask them to leave (or making up an excuse for why they need to go). I like to pick one topic to either share or ask them about and give the entire exchange five minutes. Also, never sit down—a casual lean on the door frame or into the cubicle wall gives the illusion that you are passing by instead of stopping by for a full weekend debrief.

4:30 p.m. On auction days, I have a reminder set at 4:30 p.m. and block off my calendar from 4:45 to 5:00 p.m. so that I have roughly half an hour to wind down the day, check in with my team, and address any last-minute concerns. I always tell them, "I am leaving in fifteen minutes in case you need anything from me." I try to leave my team feeling empowered so they have the answers they need to continue their work as well. That being said, there are also times when I can't get to every answer before I leave, so I don't put down my phone for the night the minute I leave the office. I continue doing emails on the subway. I am all for indulging a solid amount of time scrolling through my phone, but I set time limits on Instagram, Facebook, and Twitter to indulge my whim without it turning into a complete waste of time. Although you might be waiting in line to pick up the kids for school in your car, or waiting on a subway platform for a train, or just waiting to check out at Trader Joe's, try to use those moments to bang out anything work related instead of squandering the time liking a picture of someone you have never met on Instagram.

5:15 p.m. As I head down the hallway of my apartment building, I always finish the email that I am working on or resolve any urgent issues before I walk in the door. On more than one occasion,

I have been standing outside the door to my apartment typing an email when I've looked down to see my neighbor's little girl staring up at me quizzically: "What are you doing, Miss Lydia?" Nine times out of ten, I don't even hear her walk up to me, which shows you how absorbed I am by my phone and the issues that come with it. My kids want their mom, not the global head of strategic partnerships, when I walk in the door. And I want to see their smiling faces as they run down the hall to get a hug, not the illuminated words on my iPhone in front of me. If I have to stand outside my door for twenty minutes to make sure I am able to get offline for a couple of hours until their bedtime, I will do it. I want to be fully present with the kids from the time I get home through the time I put them to bed. Unless it is truly urgent, I am unavailable from the time I walk into my apartment until the time I close the door of my daughter's room.

After tucking my phone into my purse, I walk into the apartment and am met with the chaos of three children who are home from school and usually about to sit down for their dinner. The next two hours is all about them—hearing about their day, singing to music, dividing up bath time with our nanny so that we can wash off the fun of the day and get into pajamas. Our nanny leaves, and the rest of the evening is spent reading books and getting the kids ready for bed. By the time I finally get them into their beds between 7:00 and 7:15, I usually feel like crawling into bed too. But the minute I walk out of my older daughter's room, I am back online, and in most cases can stay on as long as necessary throughout the evening in order to finish everything that needs to be done or until my husband gets home. Even on nights when I have charity auctions, I will be answering emails in the taxi and backstage until a few minutes before I go on. The beauty and the curse of the smartphone. You can work from anywhere, anytime. But you can also work from anywhere, anytime.

7:30 p.m. No matter how exhausted I might be at this point in the day, I have to motivate myself to switch into high gear for my night job. I have already planned out what I am changing into for the auction, and I've placed everything I need (notes, gavel, lipstick) in an evening purse that is sitting by the front door, so now it is about making sure that I feel stage-ready. If you were to glance in my window around this time, you would see me standing in a half-zipped cocktail dress, attempting to curl or straighten my hair, putting on full stage makeup, and reading over my auction lots again and again to get the information lodged into my brain. I throw my heels in a bag and put on a pair of flats in case I have to get out of a taxi and run ahead because of bad traffic, and I am ready and waiting to hear the sound of the key in the front door. If I leave this until the last minute I feel stressed and flustered; if I set everything out I don't even have to think about it.

8:00 p.m. My husband arrives home just in time to zip up the back of my dress and exchange a quick debrief of the day, and I am out the door and headed to my night shift.

9:00 p.m. If I am not sitting for the dinner portion of the evening, I arrive when the program is about to begin so that I have a few minutes to quickly troubleshoot any last-minute questions or issues that may arise. Backstage, I stand reviewing notes until I hear the Voice of God: "3, 2, 1 . . ." Strike, Strike, Strike . . . "Good evening, ladies and gentleman . . ." The nerves that I feel backstage dissipate immediately once the gavel hits the podium, and I am off.

10:00 p.m. I am usually finished with the auction and on my way home by this point in the evening. I don't like to eat before auctions, so I usually end up ordering something that will be delivered around the same time that I get home, or grab something out of the fridge.

10:30 p.m. I am finally home for the night in pajamas on the couch, eating and working on my book or talking to my husband about the part of the day we didn't cover in our first five-minute encounter. If my husband is already asleep I will sit down and write or make sure everything is ready for the kids' school and double-check my schedule to anticipate anything that may arise the following day.

11:45 p.m./12:00 a.m. I try to be in bed no later than midnight, though as a child I was a night owl. My mom used to say that she worried about what I would end up doing with my life since I always seemed more excited about staying up late than getting in bed early. If I weren't facing three energetic children in the morning, I would be up until at least 2:00 or 3:00 a.m. reading a book. Or maybe writing my second book. Which is a little further down on my life road map. But as you can see, on an average day, I don't waste a minute. The day never feels stressful or out of control because I can visualize what needs to happen next and then react to any curveballs that are thrown my way.

By understanding what my day is going to look like before I walk out of the door, I end each day feeling like I have done everything I needed to do, which allows me to feel like I am succeeding at the end of most days. Not all days, but most days. Prioritizing time with my kids and my husband, accomplishing the goals that I set each day, and continuing to think about setting new goals so that I feel fulfilled—this is what success looks like to me. But that isn't the case for everyone. So figure out what success looks like to you and start to map out what it will take for you to get there. Only when you are confident in yourself and what you want will you have the clarity and focus to look ahead and figure out your next steps. And that is when you will be able to sell yourself and your vision to other people.

I know this firsthand. Five years ago, I took an auction for a nonprofit called Room to Grow at the Mandarin Oriental ballroom, an event space with stunning views of Central Park seen through a wall of windows high above Manhattan. I stood onstage next to the lithe, blond beauty Uma Thurman, who introduced me and then gave one last plea encouraging the bidders to give as much as possible to the charity. I had been the auctioneer for the Room to Grow benefit for a number of years, and early in the auction, as I bantered with the audience, my eyes fell on a gentleman in the front row wearing a pair of black-rimmed glasses who had raised his hand to bid.

As I often do when taking auctions, I immediately assigned him a persona. The persona serves a dual purpose: it helps draw people into the auction and helps me remember the bidder throughout the auction. The persona is usually the first celebrity doppelgänger who comes to mind when I look at the person. In some cases, I hold my tongue for fear of insulting the bidder, but not this time.

"Welcome to the auction, Clark Kent."

The comment drew a few laughs from the audience and a smile

from my bidder. More importantly, it didn't slow his bidding. The more he bid, the more airtime he received as part of the auction:

"Clark Kent bidding directly in front of me; writer by day, Superman by night."

"He probably changed in the phone booth on the way upstairs tonight."

"Saving the world in a red cape and a pair of tights."

Clark Kent quickly became the star of the show.

Following the auction, Clark Kent came up to me and introduced himself as Uma Thurman's agent, Jason Weinberg, founder of Untitled Entertainment, one of the top talent agencies in Los Angeles.

After a few pleasantries, he asked if I would be interested in having breakfast with Uma and him later that month to discuss what I could do with "my talent."

Internal monologue: *Are you kidding me? OH MY GOD. Play it cool. Play it cool. Don't pass out. Don't smile too much. Just smile a little. Play it cool.*

To Clark Kent and Uma: "Sure. That would be lovely. Looking forward to it."

He sent me an email later that night with one line in the heading: "I'm finding you a show."

This wasn't the first time that I had been approached after getting offstage. In fact, almost ten years into my auctioneering career, it seemed like there was always someone coming up to offer me their card or ask the same question.

What was I going to do with "my talent"? Although I would smile and say with a wink, "What? Raising half a million dollars in fifteen minutes wasn't enough for you?" if I was honest with myself, I knew exactly what they meant. I always felt like there was more to the story than me onstage night after night as an auctioneer. I have a love of selling items, pivoting from lot to lot, bidder to bidder, but it's not only that. I also love inspiring and motivating the audience. I knew there was something. I just didn't have clarity on what it was or how I was going to get there.

To be fair, many other people had come up with ideas for me:

A reality show!

No. That wasn't it. That seemed like a surefire way to bomb a solid career path within Christie's. Also, I have never been particularly good at catfighting or pulling out other people's hair.

Acting or comedy or hosting a show? It seemed no one could quite figure it out. And neither could I.

I knew that I didn't want to squander this slightly surreal opportunity, so I sat down the night before our breakfast and sketched out a road map of my career. And right there, at the top of the list, sat one of my goals:

Write a book.

The next day, Jason, Uma, and Uma's producing partner Gabrielle took me to breakfast at the Gramercy Park Hotel. As you can imagine, I spent the entire breakfast praying that someone I wanted to impress would stroll by and see that my company that morning was slightly more impressive than my usual breakfast companions grabbing coffee at Starbucks. No such luck.

Over breakfast we discussed the usual mix of ideas: host of a TV show, role on a comedy show, but then I told them about my idea to create a platform where I could teach people what I had learned selling to audiences large and small, night after night onstage around the world. I wanted to teach people how to sell as themselves, how to motivate, inspire, and form a human connection with the people in front of them.

The breakfast lasted a couple of hours. We left with a solid game plan in place. A flurry of emails, a number of meetings, but I still didn't know exactly what "it" was that I wanted to write about, and though I would write a little here and there, nothing ever seemed to come together. Ultimately, nothing came from the meeting because I hadn't fully mapped out how to get from where I was to where I wanted to be. But the seeds of the idea had been planted—I wanted to write a book. I thought about it a lot over the next few years, but I was also busy having three kids, so whenever I thought of it, I also thought about the other things that needed to be done—school applications, doctor's appointments, playdates, my full-time job. There were so many other things going on in my life that it made the thought of actually figuring out how to write a book, how to sell a book, and everything in between seem daunting. But I continued to consider what I wanted to write about and began to sketch an outline for what I wanted this book to be.

Four years after the breakfast at the Gramercy Park Hotel, it took one more breakfast to lead me even closer to my goal. After a couple of years of working with him in my role as head of strategic partnerships at Christie's, Keith Fox, the CEO of Phaidon Press, happened to attend the Hetrick-Martin Institute auction, where I was the auctioneer. It is always a lively, engaged auction, and we easily surpassed their fundraising goal, thanks to the amazing crowd. Keith emailed me the following day to set up breakfast, which was not uncommon, as we had a lot of our meetings over breakfast. I arrived at the breakfast thinking that we were about to discuss the strategy for the Christie's-Phaidon partnership, but a minute into the breakfast it was clear that Keith had something else on his mind. Without even glancing at his menu, Keith asked me the question I had heard so many times. "I want to know: What are you going to do with your talent?" The question surprised me because until that moment I hadn't thought about the fact that as the CEO of a publishing company, Keith would be the perfect person to help me figure out what to do in order to sell a book. But this time I had a road map for the book in my mind and sitting in front of me was the perfect person to ask for help. So I did just that. "I want to write a book on selling, but I have no idea where to begin." Within days Keith had introduced me to a number of friends and colleagues in the publishing industry who talked me through the bookselling and writing process. A process that once seemed daunting all of a sudden seemed doable.

I truly believe life places things in front of you at the right time, but it is only when you are open to those opportunities that things start to really happen for you. The doors that Keith opened helped me further along on my road map, but I was the one who had to come to the table with a clear vision and a direction for what I wanted. The process took years, but the momentum that those conversations started has set forth one of the most amazing new chapters of my life. And I'm just getting started.

I cannot stress enough the importance of creating a road map for all aspects of your life. To become the Most Powerful Woman in the Room, you need to know where you are headed. Sometimes I find that sitting down with a pencil and paper and simply sketching out a physical plan is the easiest way to do it. Over the course of the year, I go back to my road map time and time again to update it, add to it, make edits for unforeseen events that occur, and celebrate internally when I hit a milestone along the way.

One last thing to keep in mind. A road map has no time limit. Just because you decide that you want to finish a project in a year doesn't always mean it is going to happen. It took me five years from the first time I spoke about writing the book to writing the proposal. Once I finished the proposal, I sold it in three weeks. The first email I sent after selling the proposal was to Jason Weinberg to thank him for taking me out for breakfast almost five years ago. The second was to Keith Fox for giving me the tools to make it happen. Network or die, right?

The Most Powerful Woman in the Room goes after whatever she wants to ensure she lives the life she wants to live. She creates a road map for her personal and professional life to stay on track and moving forward. You may not get what you want every time you want it. But if you keep your eye on the prize and stay focused, you can achieve more than you ever dreamed was possible. I am sure a lot of people I know never in a million years thought that I could write a book, and maybe at one time I was one of those people too. But deep down inside I knew I would get here. Just like I know that if you dig deep, create your road map, and start moving forward, you will too.

how they roadmap their life

SIAN BEILOCK

**President of Barnard College
and Cognitive Scientist**

Life is stressful. That we know. But there are strategies we can use to ease the pressure. The greater the number of demands on me, the more I have to take stock and pay attention. And that means plotting a course, figuring out priorities with lists and charts, and committing to completion. But somewhat counterintuitively, it also means being flexible and facile enough to adapt and adjust. So I try to write my road map in pencil instead of pen and, as my research suggests, I allot time to take a break from rigidity, when needed. A ten-minute walk in nature, a quick sprint around the block, or even a few minutes of stillness to clear the brain can do the trick. Usually I find that I get where I want to go with a lot more of myself intact.

KRISTEN MORRISSEY THIEDE

Senior Vice President of Business Development
and Corporate Strategy, Starry, Inc.

In 2000 I bought advertising from Google. Every time I called to give Google more money, they would introduce me to a new contact. This happened three times before I said, "If you are hiring all these people you should hire me." They flew me to New York and I interviewed with people all day long only to learn I did not get the job. It was a new position and the internal team could not agree on what they were looking for.

I followed up two months later and asked if they ever filled the position; they said, "No. Do you want to interview again?" So I flew back to New York and interviewed again for an entire day, and again they did not give me the job. Two more months went by. The recruiter called me and asked if I wanted to interview again. I said yes, but this time I arrived in New York with a PowerPoint presentation on how I would do the job. The Google team said yes! My parents and friends at the time had no idea what Google was and thought moving to California for an online yellow pages was a terrible idea. Lucky I said yes and the rest is herstory!

KATE SCHELTER

Author of *Classic Style*, Artist, Creative Director, and Stylist

I invented myself. I drew up the plans. I invented Kate Schelter. I have carefully cultivated my career—owning Kate Schelter LLC for twenty years—by defining myself, clarifying my goals, reinventing my role(s), and by owning it completely. I can create what I can visualize, write down, or imagine.

Let's start simple: I write everything down on paper. Everything. To-do lists, food shopping, fleeting ideas, people I need to reply to, errands, professional goals, personal goals, self-care, brilliant thoughts that come to me at 3:00 a.m. during insomnia, people I want to meet, trips I want to take, exhibits to attend, dreams I want to accomplish, projects to pitch, friends I want to meet for dinner. If I think it, I can do it—all by writing it down, because the act of writing things down on paper is cathartic. Writing actually drives thoughts into my subconscious—and it often sparks ideas themselves. A woman who knows what she wants is a powerful creature because there's nothing stopping her from crossing every item off her list—she makes them happen. I keep pads of paper and pens in every room of my house—how many awesome ideas and thoughts come while flossing your teeth or doing the dishes? Jot down in a journal larger ideas, projects you long for. I don't respond to things in the same order they enter my life's inbox. I am able to PRIORITIZE my time based on what I need to do and what others need from me. There's *important* and there's *urgent*. Urgent is life and death. Everything else is prioritized according to me. My priorities become the talking points of my life—with friends, with myself in my head, with the universe. Ever notice how much you get done the day before you leave for a trip? Tackle every workday with that passion and vigilance—like the plane is departing for Tulum and it's time to board!

If you work in a visual industry, then your road map must be visual—whether it's photographs, your own drawings and sketches, plans—everything that is important and deeply personal to you belongs on that board. That you recognize these things means they are a part of you. They may need to be further cultivated and developed within your career. You're on the right track!

Cultivate all that you want by practicing it every day. Be it. Talk about it. Get it out there.

THE MOST
POWERFUL
WOMAN
IN THE
ROOM . . .

9

evolves, innovates, and connects

Tell me the truth.

Have you ever pressed the mute button on your speakerphone during a conference call or an informational interview or a call with a friend or parent to type loudly on your keyboard? To leave the room to get water or a coffee or a piece of chocolate from the candy bowl on the desk across the office when that person leaves to go to a meeting?

I have. Many, many times.

Why is this important?

Because if you have done it, chances are someone has done it to you.

As I said, technology is a wonderful thing. Especially for the hours I save thanks to FreshDirect, Uber, and the Starbucks app.

BUT.

It also makes tuning people out far too easy. And when you are trying to sell, the human connection—and understanding the objectives of the person you are selling to—is the piece that can make or break your pitch. The crucial part of selling anything is understanding what the person on the other side of the table wants and how whatever you are selling can help them achieve that goal. You have to know your audience. If you want to think about this in opposite terms, think about the telemarketer who calls you and launches into their pitch before you can even answer their question "How you are doing today?" and amid so much ambient background noise that you might as well be in the call center with them. It is part of the script they are reading so that they can dive right into their pitch. They don't really care about how you are doing; nor do you believe that they care about how you are doing. But by forcing you to engage, they get you to commit to at least the next five seconds of the pitch.

If you don't believe me, try this approach on a friend you suspect might have you on mute. It is nearly impossible to mute someone who is asking you pertinent questions without being downright rude. It's much easier to mute someone who is bulldozing through a checklist of points they need to cover without pausing to take the temperature of the person they are pitching to on the other end of the line. You know how you click on a dress that you like online and then it ends up on every webpage you visit for the rest of the day? The clothing company is engaging you in a dialogue of sorts. Once they see that you like something, they come back to you, and then they change the conversation—they lower the price, they remind you that something is still in your basket to purchase, they lower the price again. When you are pitching face-to-face, you are doing the same thing, except that you have the benefit of knowing whether or not things are crashing and burning in front of you. When I first started strategic partnerships, I used to go to pitches with a number in mind for what I wanted the outside company to pay for access to Christie's. But what I quickly realized is that pitching is rarely as black-and-white as I used to make it seem. Selling can have many shades of gray, and unless you are willing to hear what the other person has to say, you might as well leave the minute you finish your pitch. Oftentimes the number that I am looking for does not line up with what the other company has budgeted for certain partnerships. However, if I can convince them to look at it from a different angle—perhaps incorporating elements from other programs that could be paid for by advertising and marketing budgets instead of the smaller events budget—I can find different ways to hit my target. It is a little like playing chess: the moves might be different each game, but the objective is always the same. In my case, if the company doesn't have the budget that I am looking for, there are times when I can redirect the conversation toward something more appropriate for their budget. It is always better for me to understand the parameters of their budget before even opening my mouth so that I don't shut down the conversation before it starts. Selling is not about telling someone what you want to tell them. It is understanding their objective and tailoring your pitch to make whatever you are selling meet their goals. Instead of walking into a meeting thinking about what you are going to get from them, try to make your offer help them reach their objectives. There is always a point of synergy, and your job is to find it.

First and foremost, whenever possible, try to meet someone face-to-face and make your pitch in person. Revolutionary? No. But I guarantee you that meeting someone face-to-face will lay the groundwork for a solid foundation. It's a chance to get to know someone on a human level outside of titles and office caste systems—and, most importantly, away from a device that allows them to do other things while you are speaking. There is no doubt that the partnerships where I have taken the time to get to know the other team and understand where they are coming from have proved more dynamic and fruitful than those where everything took place over the phone or on email. Any working relationship is good during good times, but it is during the times when things are going off the rails that a better understanding of the people you are working with helps you get through in a collaborative way rather than spending time pointing fingers.

Aren't you more likely to give someone the benefit of the doubt or refrain from firing off a terse email if you know the person who will be the recipient? I certainly am. Receiving an email from Caroline, who I know has just had twin boys who are currently on sleep strike, is going to resonate more than an email coming from xxxx@gmail.com, whom I have never met. I also find that people are more likely to do business with you if they enjoy spending time with you and vice versa. I have had partnerships extend a year or two past the expected timeline simply because our teams loved collaborating so much that we kept inventing new ways to work together. Much to my husband's chagrin, I am not much of a golfer, but I fully understand how spending a four- to five-hour chunk of a day golfing is a good business idea. You can learn a lot about someone over a four-hour period. Without a doubt, the best partnerships that I have created at Christie's have worked because we get along with the people on the other team.

Best-case scenario, you have a chance to meet in person. However, if face-to-face isn't possible, there are ways to form a connection without the need for a plane or train ticket. Here are four tips to crush it every time you are asked to pitch anything over the phone:

1. Research the person you are calling and then spend the first two minutes of a call getting to know the person on the other end of the line.

   Organize your calls at the beginning of the day so that you get someone when they are feeling fresh and rested and hopefully in control of their day. Whenever possible, use technology to set you up for success before you even get on the phone. Google the person you are about to speak with and find any natural points of connectivity that can help you relate to that person. Then try to spend the first couple of minutes of a call learning as much as you can about the person that you are speaking with before starting the formal part of the call. I'm not talking about ten minutes of casual conversation—be respectful of their time and the time allotted for the call—but spend time learning a little bit about the person. Keep notes about anything that person tells you about family, trips, etc., so you can bring it up again the next time you speak. A talented salesperson will use personal information as ammunition to engage their prospect and then continually re-engage them throughout the conversation.

   It is the same thing on email. If you are trying to get the attention of someone via email, make sure to do research on them in the same way that you would research someone for an informational interview. Try to find a shared background (we grew up in the same state, we have been in our companies for the same number of years) that makes the pitch personal, and then keep it brief and to the point. Most people have short attention spans these days, given the number of things on their to-do list, so don't add to it, but instead show that you have spent time above and beyond the five seconds it takes to cut and paste.

2. Get off Instagram, Snapchat, and Twitter.

Whether you are the person making the pitch or listening to the pitch, shut your computer and put any other mobile devices away in a drawer or in your purse. This is advice coming from someone who loves to multitask with the best of them. But when I am listening to a pitch or pitching to someone, I try to remove any distractions so that I can be totally immersed in what the person on the other line is saying. If I am trying to do too many things at once, I can easily miss important things that would be beneficial either later on in that conversation or any future conversations. Ask any member of my team; one of the first things that I do before a meeting is turn my computer screen toward the wall. I find it so hard to pay attention to the person in front of me when emails are popping up in Outlook, but I also had a boss who used to check email while I was talking and it drove me insane. I never felt confident that I was able to make my point because it never seemed like I had her full attention. I always left wondering if she had actually heard anything that I said over the course of the conversation or if she was ordering groceries online while I spoke to her.

3. Mirror, mirror, on the wall.

Whenever I am meeting with a nonprofit about an upcoming auction or a new company for the first time, I always ask if there is an acronym or a nickname for the organization that I can use to make the person in front of me or the audience feel like I am part of their squad. Same thing with a pitch. Try to immediately familiarize yourself with the language that they are using and pitch in the same language. To be clear, I don't mean try to speak Spanish if they are speaking Spanish, but if you find that the person on the other end of the line likes to pepper you with business-school buzzwords like "cascade," "verticals," and "SWOT analysis," or if a nonprofit uses an acronym instead of their full name, feel free to reuse their words when you are pitching your message back to them by phone or by email.

4. Pivot, pivot, pivot.

One thing to always remember when you are speaking over the phone or in person is that you will have the opportunity to craft your pitch in real time. A good thing to remember when you are trying to succeed in any type of sale, whether it be selling yourself in an interview or selling your idea or concept, is to constantly mold your discussion so that it feels like a two-sided conversation instead of a monologue. After you begin the initial part of the conversation, spend time listening to what the person opposite you is saying about their objectives. Whenever there is a natural point of connectivity, try to weave your point into the conversation so that there is a nice back-and-forth dialogue throughout.

In order to remain relevant in sales, it will always be important that you stay in the know about the various platforms and technology that you can use to help enhance your selling ability. Because sometimes it is the convergence of human connection and technology that makes for the most effective way to sell. Years ago I took an auction in San Francisco for Tipping Point, an organization aimed at ending poverty in the Bay Area. The audience was made up of San Francisco's biggest donors: a perfect blend of philanthropic San Franciscans and engaged donors from the Silicon Valley community. In addition to having donors from the tech world, the auction was attended by many people who work in technology, so they always have the latest and greatest in both their visual technology and their bidding technology. For instance, when I took the auction this year I took bids in cryptocurrency. The format for the auction is fairly simple: a short live auction of two or three lots followed by a paddle raise. It is always fun to take an auction in a city other than New York, because I get the benefit of a fresh audience, and cities outside New York tend to have fewer galas, so audiences don't have auction fatigue after attending one every night of the week.

I had heard fantastic things about the generosity of the Tipping Point community, and to my delight the crowd did not disappoint. From the first auction lot to the final lot, hands flew in the air and the bidding flew past the expected prices to two, three, and then four times what we were hoping to earn. It was clear to me from the stage that the audience was connected, engaged, and incredibly motivated to give to an organization they felt could make a change in their community. Following the auction, the CEO and I stood onstage for the paddle-raise portion of the evening. As I had seen at plenty of auctions in New York that spring, there was a growing trend away from the traditional paddle raise. These days many companies in the auction space market auction devices that are essentially iPhones for paddle raises so that guests can make their donation anonymously without raising their hand or engaging in the paddle-raise banter. When the devices first came onto the auction scene about five years ago, every organization seemed to want to try them or would ask if I could do the paddle raise in tandem with the devices. It seemed like a good idea at first—certainly it would make the back end easier for the organization. But after only a few auctions, from my vantage point onstage I could see that the paddle raise seemed flat when it was left to a device, and time and time again I would hear from an organization that the results weren't as good as they had been when they were using a live auctioneer. Many of the organizations that I have worked with over the years moved toward using the digital technology to enhance their paddle raise and then ultimately moved back to a live auctioneer to execute the paddle-raise portion of the evening.

The two most marked things I noticed from the stage when this movement toward digital giving began? First, the minute you allow anyone in the room to pick up their phone, they immediately disconnect from the experience that they were previously engaged in. In addition, nine out of ten times, even if the guests have good intentions and are planning to donate, when they pick up their phone and see an email from work or their latest match on Tinder, they forget all about the donation and start swiping away. Net-net: no donation and no engagement. Second, it sucks the energy out of the room. All that great energy from your community is simply gone. Instead of building on the energy of a room to push your paddle raise to a higher level, you are basically staring at people as they stare at their phones. They are having a full-on relationship, but it's just with their phone. In the case of Tipping Point, a lot of things digitally enhanced the experience for a person donating on their phone—there was a large screen with graphics that grew and grew as the donations continued. But from my perspective, I felt like the room would do more if people were engaged watching their peers give generously. I could already see that this was an audience that was motivated to give; I wanted the chance to see what the crowd would do if they were motivated as a community instead of individuals. Is there anything as motivating as good old-fashioned peer pressure that is working for a great cause? The only thing better is peer pressure for a great cause with an auctioneer pushing you to give the most that you can possibly give. And that's where I come in.

The Tipping Point auction raises over ten million dollars every year on the night of the benefit, and we can all agree that you never want to mess with a formula that is working that well. But after working with Tipping Point for a couple of years, I was certain that a paddle raise with a highly motivated crowd that had the same high energy as their blockbuster live auction would yield even greater results. As I said, it never hurts to ask. The worst anyone can say is no.

A few weeks later, I had a call with the Tipping Point team about the upcoming auction. They were planning to have only one live lot in the auction and told me that they felt uncomfortable asking me to fly across the country to take one live auction lot followed by a paddle raise where people were giving using handheld devices. It was the opening I needed. I suggested that they move away from the paddle raise as a purely digital moment and back to a good old-fashioned paddle raise. I asked them to let me take it the way that I had been taking it for ten years—as a live giving moment. We went back and forth about whether the crowd would go for it, because they hadn't been thrilled with that approach in the past, and they finally agreed to let me give it a try. But the beauty of Tipping Point is that while they were amenable to letting me take the paddle raise the old-school way, they also worked to find a new type of technology that would still allow for the immediate charge to the bidder so they didn't lose a second when recording their information. So when guests entered the event, instead of receiving a device that made people look down, they were given a bracelet that they wore on their wrist to raise high into the air when they wanted to bid. A volunteer would simply touch their device to the bracelet and voilà, the bidder who had been registered when they walked in the door now had a lot less money, but Tipping Point had a lot more.

The night of the auction I felt nervous but kept my poker face intact—half of being a leader is committing to a plan and following through. I sensed that their team felt a little nervous, especially given the incredible amount of money that their paddle raise brings in every year, but to their credit they were fully supportive when I walked onto the stage.

In the program leading up to the live auction, a Tipping Point client spoke about how she had benefited from the organization's work. She told a painful story of life with a mother who would take her out of school to make the mom's begging on the street seem more compelling; she spoke of bouncing from house to house before finally being adopted by a couple who set her up for success. One part of her speech brought me to tears as I waited backstage: she spoke of moving in with her adopted parents and their expectations that she act appropriately, commit to her lessons in school, and respect the house that she was living in. She simply said, "When people expect you to do something, you follow through." Lesson number three: Mirror the language that you hear people using. When I went out onto the stage to do the paddle raise, I immediately picked up the phrase that had caught my attention from the speech. Expectation. "I *expect* you to raise the money that I am asking for in this paddle raise." There were 1,300 people in the audience, and they raised their hands faster than I could take down the numbers. The energy was high, the people were cheering for one another, and Tipping Point not only raised the amount that they wanted, but they crushed their goal. Tipping Point has one of the most enthusiastic, engaged audiences in the charity auctioneering world—it was such a privilege to help them raise the money needed to continue their mission to end poverty in the Bay Area.

Following the auction, a group of guys sought me out and started firing questions at me about my job as an auctioneer. They wanted to know how I was able to get so much money out of the crowd, etc. A question one of them asked that stuck with me was, "How could we write an algorithm for what you are doing on-stage during the paddle raise?" There are many things that can be replaced by a tablet or a smartphone, but when it comes to selling, you cannot replace the human connection. Yet at the same time, as the world continues to evolve, it is imperative that you evolve with it and find ways to work with technology to enhance your selling ability.

The Most Powerful Woman in the Room is constantly evolving and innovating to keep up with our rapidly changing world. Being nimble and accepting change is what leaders do. This doesn't mean that you can't integrate that human connection into the tech-filled life that you are living today. In this constantly changing world, it is important to find ways to utilize technology to enhance your sales, but never forget what makes it impactful. You.

how they evolve and innovate
in their lives

MEENA HARRIS

Founder, Phenomenal Woman Campaign

Pay attention to what's right in front of you. Pour yourself into it—as though it's the single most important thing in the world. If you think creatively, act boldly, and work really hard, chances are it will take you places. Last year, when I launched the Phenomenal Woman Action Campaign, it was supposed to be a small thing: a one-month digital campaign side project. Today—a year and a half later—we've reached a digital audience of more than 286 million, and we're still going strong. I didn't set out to start a movement; my plan had always been to return to my day job in the tech industry, or at a law firm. But once it took off, the question became: how can we do even more—keep growing, reach new people, have a bigger impact?

It's never easy, and no outcome is guaranteed. Sometimes you fail, or you don't execute on the best idea, or you find that every step forward is accompanied by two steps back. But so long as you stick with your passions and learn from your missteps, then—as the great Dolores Huerta once said—"Every moment is an organizing opportunity, every person a potential activist, every minute a chance to change the world."

KAREN SPENCER

Founder & CEO, Whole Child International

As a social entrepreneur focused on transforming the childcare system for vulnerable children, innovation, connection, and evolution are at the top of my mind. I actually think of myself first and foremost as an innovator. I have learned that one of the most crucial elements to being a successful innovator is embracing the inevitable failures that come along the way. The kiss of death for innovation in any area is being too attached to your ideas. It requires the ability to believe enough in your vision that you can connect on every level, with your team, your partners, and funders in order to get what you need. At the same time, we must have the flexibility and openness to see where our thinking was flawed. *That* is where great discovery is possible. We need to be steadfast and determined, and also open and flexible. At the end of the day, our power lies in the ability to believe in our ideas and create solutions that move our ideas forward, connecting all the dots when the inevitable failure appears, regrouping, and beginning again. Evolution.

THE MOST
POWERFUL
WOMAN
IN THE
ROOM . . .

10

catches more bees with honey, but honey, don't mess with a southern woman

If you know anything about southern women, you know they have a way with words. In particular, they have one-liners with so many layers it can make your head spin. My grandmother was no exception. A southern belle through and through, she drove a Cadillac, never got out of her car unless one of her sons walked around the car and opened the door for her, and went to the beauty salon at least three times a week to ensure there was never a hair out of place. She was the queen of the one-liner, and she delivered them with an arched eyebrow and a twinkle in her eye. Anytime she would hear one of her children or grandchildren say something with a sharpness of tone, she would smile knowingly and say, "You catch more bees with honey." If my grandmother had her master's degree in catching bees with honey, it is fair to say that my mother has her PhD. As a child, I regularly watched two generations of women on the charm offensive. To this day, no one stands a chance.

Lessons that seemed trite and silly when my southern grandmother mentioned them to me as a child have become examples that have served me well over the course of my life—in life *and* in business. So, if you didn't have a southern grandmother dressed to the nines with a pocketbook and a matching pair of shoes to guide you, and a British mother who has lived longer in the South than she lived in England, here are a few lessons I learned from growing up in the South that will help you in your quest to become the Most Powerful Woman in the Room.

Lesson #1: Always write a thank-you note.

After the thrill of Christmas Day in our house—unwrapping gifts, mountains of delicious food and sweets, catnaps due to the aforementioned food—there was always the dreaded ritual the day after . . . the day when we had to write thank-you notes to all of our relatives who had sent Christmas presents. With a British mother and a southern father, my siblings and I had no chance of avoiding this tradition. After copious amounts of grumbling, the four of us would sit at the dining room table and scratch out our thank-you notes in increasingly large handwriting to fill up the notes as quickly as possible. Inevitably, there would be the moment when my mother would come in to remind us that we should be able to fit more than five words per page, whereupon we would all groan and start again with normal-size handwriting until she came back with another reminder.

For many years, I wrote thank-you notes simply because the alternative was getting grounded, but as I grew up, I began to enjoy writing them. I have a few close friends who still write exceptionally good thank-you notes. Even when people send a quick text or email as a thank-you, I still love picking up our mail and seeing a beautiful colored envelope standing out against the rest of the white letter-size mail. There is something to be said for opening a card or a short note that shows someone went out of their way to sit down and thank you for your time or a dinner, or even just to say hi.

Over the years I have realized that while the art of writing thank-you notes may be forgotten to many, people certainly do not forget you if you can write a good thank-you note. In my twenties, I began to take the time to write a few extra lines that went above and beyond just "Thank you for the . . ." and throwing in a line or two about what I was doing in life. Friends of my in-laws still remind me about the thank-you notes I sent after my wedding. I spent a little time thinking about each person, how I knew them, and what I could mention that might be of interest about our lives. Same with my baby showers, and now I am the person making our kids write thank-you notes for their birthday presents. You might be wondering what writing a thank-you note has to do with becoming the Most Powerful Woman in the Room, but, as a manager, I would never hire someone to work on my team if they didn't send a thank-you note following an interview. I will take an email thank-you note, but I always prefer to receive a handwritten note.

When I became the director of special events for Christie's Americas at the age of twenty-six, I knew a lot of the senior leaders were wondering if I had what it took to run a department producing five hundred events a year with a team of only three people. One thing was for sure: I had seen plenty of examples of how I did not want to act as a leader on my team. As the intern, coordinator, and manager of the department, I had certainly seen sides of external event planners, internal colleagues, and clients that I had no interest in replicating. Events can be stressful, because every event has a deadline you are up against. And I had watched as completely rational people became unglued, high-strung, excitable, rude, or pushy in the days and hours leading up to a big event. It all trickled down from the top. If the person in charge is losing their cool, you had better believe that everyone working for them is doing exactly the same thing. Not only was I not interested in acting in that manner, but I didn't want my team acting like that to other people.

I found myself hiring southern women in those early years. It wasn't hard to pinpoint exactly what it was about the women who came to interview: the accent, the accommodating manner that seemed both polished and professional, the ability to work seamlessly with our clients no matter the level of wealth or status. I found that hiring southern women for positions in my team came with unexpected benefits—the way they dealt with difficult clients, the graciousness that came out whenever there were issues that needed kid gloves, and the fact that they all wrote thank-you notes on monogrammed stationery. Because something about being from the South means your monogram is on every single thing you own. Especially your stationery.

Shortly after I took over the department, a friend from college called to ask if I would meet his sister-in-law to secure her a place in the Christie's summer internship program, which I did. After she started her internship, she would check in occasionally, and as it came to an end we agreed to grab lunch. Over the course of the lunch, it was clear that she was smart and driven, and as we were finishing up the meal, she came out of left field with a one-liner about something she had observed at Christie's that showed there was more to her than her résumé implied. Nothing quite like a quick wit to win me over. What did I say about being southern? A lot of layers. At the end of the meal, she reminded me that she would be returning to college that year, but asked that I keep her in mind for a job should there ever be an availability in my department.

After we agreed to stay in touch, she went back to college and I went back to work, assuming I would hear from her around graduation time the next year and could hopefully help her find a job either within Christie's or outside Christie's. But over the course of the year, she would sporadically send a note, on her mono- grammed stationery, reminding me of her intention of coming to work on my team when she graduated. I would read the note and leave it on my desk for a few days, as a reminder for me to email to let her know that we didn't have any positions available, and then put it in my desk drawer along with the others . . . slowly growing into a small stack. Despite my belief there wouldn't be a job in my department, it impressed me that she took time out from her college days to sit and pen a note. I appreciated her thoughtfulness and the fact that she made her intentions clear. As she neared her college graduation date, she sent one last note reminding me of her upcoming graduation and once more mentioning her desire to work on my team. I left the note on my desk as a reminder to follow up with her and connect her with a few friends.

Then a funny thing happened. The next morning, one of my rock star team members put a meeting on my calendar. It wasn't unusual—there is always something that needs to be covered one- on-one out of earshot of the larger office. Truly I didn't think any- thing of it at the time, nor did I think anything of it when she came in with a slightly scared look on her face. I was early enough in my career that I didn't know what that face meant, but now, having been around the block a few times, I can spot that face from a mile away. It is the "I am leaving the company, but I am scared to tell you, so I am hoping you can guess what I am about to say so that I don't have to say it" face. She walked into the office and launched into a dialogue about her upcoming wedding and their joint decision to move to Indianapolis for her husband's job. It is exactly the kind of news you never want to hear from a high-performing team member. After giving her a hug and telling her how much I wished the best for them, I sat at my desk with my wheels spinning. There is nothing fun about trying to replace a solid member of your team; the time spent training a new person alone is enough to make anyone want to throw their head on their desk in despair.

Over the next week, as I sat at my desk running through potential candidates and wondering if it was too early for a glass of wine, my eyes drifted downward to a monogrammed note sitting on top of my desk. There sat her note in her perfect handwriting with the message she had sent many times over the course of the year. She was looking for a job in my department. Guess what? I was now looking for someone to fill a job in the department. Her graduation would coincide perfectly with my team member's departure. I would need to promote the woman who was currently working in the junior position, but the newly graduated former intern would be a perfect person to join the team. I emailed her that morning, she responded immediately, and after a few phone interviews, she moved to New York and started working in special events at Christie's, eventually taking over my position when I started strategic partnerships. When you are overseeing a team that interfaces with the wealthiest and most influential individuals in the world, you want to ensure the people representing your company and your department have a strong sense of manners.

My mother always told me that I should never show up to a party empty-handed. Her rationale was simple: "Would anyone ever be upset if you show up to their house with a gift to thank them for having you over to dinner?" Similarly, will anyone ever be upset if you sent a note thanking them for taking time out of their busy day to meet with you? No. Take a minute to stop and show appreciation for the greatest gift that someone can give you: their time. It is a simple act, but sometimes the simple acts are the ones that help you achieve your biggest goals in life.

Lesson #2: Get up, dress up, and show up.

Growing up in the South, and particularly in my house, dressing up was as important as going to church on Sunday. By "important," I mean nonnegotiable. It seemed like my parents were always getting dressed up to go out for dinner or to parties, and I never saw my grandmother dressed in anything but a dress, hair curled, sprayed, and set in place. As a child, I spent hours pulling dresses from the dress-up trunk at the end of my bed, swanning around in oversize party dresses, pilfering heels from my mother's closet, and "borrowing" lipstick tubes from her vanity whenever my friends came over to play. Though I wore a uniform through my elementary school years, one of the things I loved about both my boarding school experience at Taft and my college experience at Sewanee was that both schools had a dress code. Coat and tie for men; skirts, dresses, or nice pants for women. People always look at me like I am crazy when I tell them I went to a college where people dress up for class, but at Sewanee, which is the University of the South, it seems like the natural thing to do. If people wear dresses to football games, why wouldn't they wear them to class?

After entering the working world, I no longer had a college manual telling me I had to dress up to go to work. But I had a vision of what a working woman was supposed to look like. So I would put on a nice dress and a scarf, or a skirt and a top, and head to work dressed the way that I thought I was supposed to dress. Living in New York is amazing for many reasons, but one of the things I truly love is how you can see fashions evolve on the city streets. Pre-Instagram, I could tell what the upcoming fashion season would bring simply by walking to work every morning. The same could be said for my office. My dress code has evolved the longer I've worked at Christie's. It began with what I expected everyone to wear—suits and scarves—but the art world is filled with creatives, and our clients have money to spend on fashion, so I've been exposed to fashion at the highest level as well as fashion I could afford from less expensive places around the city.

While some would complain about having to get dressed up, I wanted to dress up. I don't dress for other people. I dress for myself. I love putting together a well-coordinated outfit with bags and shoes that complement each other but don't exactly match. Does everyone like my taste? Don't know, don't care. But while I don't care if people like that I specifically picked out a bag and shoes to match, as my grandmother would have advised, I do want them to know I care about them enough to dress up.

Dressing up is my armor. On days when I have a big pitch

or an important meeting, you better believe that whatever I am wearing makes me feel like a million bucks. The first day I was promoted to head of events at Christie's, I wore a black suit to work. I don't know why I chose a black suit, but I think something about it felt like armor. Like I could take on this next level of responsibility and demand to be taken seriously. No one told me to wear a suit, none of the other women were wearing suits, but I work in a company where people dress up for work, and I wanted to feel like I was at the top of my game. I always feel that way when I have spent time getting ready. I take things more seriously when I come dressed for the occasion. And I never worry about being overdressed. Ever. I would always rather be overdressed than underdressed. You've heard the saying "Dress for the job that you want, not the job you have," but I disagree. You should be dressing for what you want your whole life, whether your job is in an office, a volunteer position in a nonprofit, your home, or a combination of those places.

I took an auction a couple of years ago for a nonprofit I had worked with for a while. The year prior I had worn a beautiful Carolina Herrera dress I had borrowed from my friend with just enough sparkle to catch the light when I was walking around on stage. The dress is easy and comfortable, and at that point the full skirt perfectly hid the early stages of my second pregnancy. When I dashed up to the event venue the following year, I had a four-month-old baby at home. My look was less about sparkle and more about a little black dress that zipped over my nursing bra. The young event organizer smiled as I was taking off my coat and said, "We were just wondering what you were going to wear this year after that great dress you wore last year." It was clear from her face as I handed her my coat that she found this muted dress a little disappointing. It was probably the last time I wore a basic black dress onstage without at least some embellishment. I wasn't offended by what she said; I agreed with what she said. But I also gave myself a hall pass, because I had a four-month-old at home, so they were lucky that I wasn't covered in spit-up.

On nights when I am lying next to my sleeping children, knowing I have to get up and put on a full face of makeup and a cocktail dress after a whole day of work in order to take an auction, putting on a fabulous dress or an oversize pair of earrings is half the battle. Once I am in a great dress, an oversize piece of jewelry, and a pair of heels, my mood immediately lifts. I feel armed for my battle—in this case, the stage. I dress to sell, to perform, to sparkle on the stage. I wear what I wear because it makes me who I want to be at that moment, just as I put on pajamas when I get home, because that makes me ready to go to bed. Different industries have different dress codes, but never be afraid to be the person who takes the initiative to be a little more dressed up than everyone else. The Most Powerful Woman in the Room is the woman who wants to be noticed. For all the right reasons.

Lesson #3: Stop b*tching and start fixing.

You know that person in your life or your office environment who always comes to you when they have a problem? Well, as my southern friends would say, "Stop b*tching and start fixing." I have always had a great relationship with my bosses. Always. Twenty years and counting. Ask anyone who has managed me at Christie's and they will tell you the same thing. Hard worker, positive attitude, gets along with others. I have had consistently great performance reviews throughout my entire career. Why? Because if I have a problem, I don't make it my boss's problem. I either fix it and never mention it, or I come up with a solution to fix it before I approach him or her about it and enlist their help instead of laying the problem at their feet.

I have managed more than nine teams at Christie's. Can I tell you the people I enjoy managing the most? The people who have a good attitude, do everything in their power not to stir up workplace drama, and, most importantly, seek solutions instead of dwelling on problems. You don't get along with Susie who works in another department? Truthfully, it's none of my business. Don't create drama about it so that I get involved with your drama while managing my full-time job . . . and my second job. Trust me, I get plenty of drama of my own with my three little kids.

In my early twenties, I wasn't immune to the allure of office gossip. After a particularly long day, and in a particularly feisty mood, I mentioned to my boss, the head of events at the time, that I'd had an argument with this woman and that woman, and heard that this woman did this, and wasn't she just the worst? My boss paused for a minute, looked at me, and said kindly, "I like to think that if you have one argument over the course of the day, the blame could go either way, but if you have more than one argument, you should probably look in the mirror."

Gulp. Total gut check. In truth, a lot of it was me. I was one of the ones creating the drama in my work environment—and not only creating it, but helping to stir the pot. Not only in the office, but also in life. If I heard gossip, I was happy to pass it along, knowingly fueling the fire. It definitely made the workday go faster, and it was always fun to be the first one to know something that no one else knew. But you know what else it did?

It made me feel kind of awful inside. Because being hurtful and mean is never a good feeling. Think about how many times over the course of the day you are the person who is "right" and how everyone else is always "wrong." Your attitude and approach might be part of the problem.

The next time you find yourself standing outside the door to your boss's office, poised to unload a torrent of criticism about a colleague or whine about an issue you are having with a client, try a different tactic. Turn around, walk back to your desk, figure out a solution, and fix it. No one likes a whiner or a complainer, but everyone likes someone who comes at problems with a can-do attitude and a willingness to find a solution.

Lesson #4: Never let them see you sweat
(or perspire, as we say in the South).

I'll let you in on a little secret about running events at the world's leading auction business. You see the most glamorous, elegant side of people as they sip champagne and gaze at multimillion-dollar pieces of art, but you also see people completely lose their cool at the prospect of sitting next to an art-world rival or at a table they don't perceive as A-list. Events turn completely calm, rational people into frantic, irrational people. As the person in charge of the event, you are the only one who stands in the way of total chaos, and if you are like me, you quickly realize what you need is an unflappable disposition and a perfect poker face. If you are the person running the entire evening and you completely lose it, so does everyone else. The reality of event planning is that while you spend months planning things in excruciating detail, everything can be overturned at the last minute because of cancellations, unexpected guests showing up with an RSVP, catering mishaps, fire alarms, etc. As a result, you always have to be prepared to put on a smile and make everyone believe that everything is fine.

There is no question that my southern upbringing taught me to bring a smile to every problem, no matter how dramatic. Over and over again I have realized what a huge asset it is when something goes wrong. It is also a skill that I rely on time and time again as an auctioneer. I can't tell you how many times an event organizer has come running up to me while I am onstage because of a mid-auction crisis. Instead of letting myself get worked up with her as she whispers loudly in my ear, I always keep a huge smile on my face so that the audience assumes we are having a little sidebar. The crowd doesn't need to know that the auction lot bidder for the earlier lot was overserved and wanted to renege on the bidding any more than I want to tell them. As my grandmother would say, it doesn't matter how hot it gets in the kitchen, never let them see you perspire.

Lesson #5: You catch more bees with honey, but honey, don't mess with a southern woman.

I am a firm believer that you will get a lot more done in your life if you navigate through life building loyalty instead of ripping people down. If you are a leader who brings people along with them as you rise to the top of your company or your PTA or your community, people will have your back when it matters. A rising tide floats all boats, but you have to ensure you have a good relationship with the boats around you so that you can all work together. As I have mentioned a number of times in this book, I have worked at my company for twenty years. I have watched the art market expand and contract more times than I care to remember. I have also watched the staff in my workplace come and go more times than I care to remember. The one constant is that the people who lead by fear or gossip or hateful behavior will eventually either lose their job or leave. It may take a while, but I can tell you that every person who led with one of those qualities in my company is no longer there.

When I was promoted to head of events at twenty-six, there was a steep learning curve to get up to speed on the intricacies of my new job. It is a bizarre feeling when one day you have someone above you making all the decisions and then that person leaves and everyone looks to you to make the final decisions. What I didn't realize when I was the newest team member in my department, hoping I would get promoted, is you assume that the jobs above you are easy because, if you are working for good people, they make it look effortless. When senior management asked me if I would be interested in the position or if I thought they should look externally, I jumped at the chance to take the job. I remember being in a meeting shortly after my promotion when someone asked about the special events strategy for the following year. I was staring at my notes and, after about fifteen seconds of silence, the head of business development looked over and said, "Lydia, the question is for you." I realized very quickly that, good or bad, the buck would now stop with me. No one was in front of me, which is good if you are crushing it, but bad if everything is going wrong. In my case, I was just trying to keep my poker face intact long enough to figure out what I didn't know about the job and make everyone believe I knew what I was doing.

At the time, I had one team member and had just hired another to fill both the manager and coordinator positions, which had been vacated. In addition to the team members, I also had an intern. There is a special place in my heart for Christie's interns, since I started my career as one, and so I was always happy to include her in our activities to make her feel like part of the team. A couple of months after I started in my new position, I landed from a quick trip to LA to a voicemail from my intern. I always treat interns like they are part of the team, and this intern was particularly precocious, so I wasn't entirely shocked that she had called me. In the voicemail she told me she had overheard one of the women on my team telling someone in the company I was in over my head. The woman wasn't entirely wrong, as I had confided in her because we were friends, but I also knew that she was doing it to undercut my authority, presumably so she could take the job if I was fired. The only flaw in her plan was she had less experience than I did. Also, she should never have made the comments while her door was wide open and my trusty unpaid intern with whom I had a great relationship was sitting five feet away. I was livid. I was aware that I didn't know everything about the job, but I was a quick study and felt I had already mastered most of the new position in a few short months. I put a meeting on her calendar for the next day and spent the evening calming down and figuring out exactly what I wanted to say to her.

The next day, in an even tone, I told her what I had heard and gave her two choices: (1) get on this train and we figure this out together while supporting each other and growing this department; or (2) leave the station—I will find someone to replace you. Not only did she get on the train, but in the years that followed our conversation, she became one of my most loyal team members and friends.

Even if you will never use the word "y'all," know what it takes to make a good gumbo, or understand the obsession with SEC football, the Most Powerful Woman in the Room knows that southern women come to the table with their own unique skill set that can be leveraged and utilized by anyone. Feel free to borrow these lessons, no matter where you grew up. And remember, don't ever mess with a southern woman.

how their upbringing has
impacted their business

EMILIE RUBINFELD

President, Carolina Herrera

Never underestimate the power of a well-dressed woman! I've always believed in the importance of professional elegance and polished style for women in business. Building a career is a step-by-step evolution—from one day to the next, and preparing for each day like it matters and dressing up for each new day as an opportunity to seize! I try to dress as if every day (of my career) is a special occasion and as the leader I envision myself to be.

I've enjoyed a two-decade career in women's fashion and now, in my dream job, I lead a fashion brand founded by a woman who lives every day perfectly dressed with a sophistication and poise beyond compare. Having worked with the iconic American designer Carolina Herrera for many years, I can say she is the absolute embodiment of this philosophy—dressing for success impeccably every single day and commanding the attention in every room she occupies. So to that I say: use fashion and personal style to get yourself exactly where you want to go!

CATHERINE HERNANDEZ-BLADES

Senior Vice President, Chief Brand
and Communications Officer, Aflac

Southern women are abundantly gifted when it comes to charm, which often leads to being underestimated. That is always an advantage for us, at work and at play. Early in my career, I spent eighteen months as executive director of the Louisiana Seafood Promotion and Marketing Board, housed in, of all places, the Department of Wildlife and Fisheries, making me the youngest gubernatorial appointee since Reconstruction.

While others were busy talking about my shoes, specifically the fact that I would wear high heels on everything from a seaplane to an airboat, no one seemed to notice that the state legislature doubled my budget while every other department was being cut, or the other incredible results being achieved for the state's $2 billion industry. If there are lessons in this story, they are these: When dealing with a southern lady, it's best not to confuse charm with complacency, or a smile with simplemindedness. And remember, for a steel magnolia, style and substance are not mutually exclusive. In fact, it's our license to operate. Bottom line: don't let the high heels fool you!

MORGAN HUTCHINSON

Founder and CEO, BURU

More often than not, if you sell something, then you are also buying something. Perhaps it's inventory from your manufacturer or a service that makes your business more efficient—but chances are, if you're not dishing out the "honey," you're not winning. In the clothing business, I rely heavily on my manufacturers and sample makers. Throughout the process, life happens and delays occur. Are they problematic? Yes. Does yelling help? Absolutely not. Think about it like this—if the production line is backed up, who is more likely to make it to the front of the line? An angry person who barks orders or a "honey-filled" person offering up some fresh biscuits to the entire crew when the work is complete? Bottom line: Be kind. Be strong. Bring the biscuits. (A side of honey to dip them in never hurts . . .)

THE MOST
POWERFUL
WOMAN
IN THE
ROOM . . .

11

is only as good as her word

When I was a little girl, I had a penchant for stretching the truth. A lot. Not that I was the only one, mind you, but I spent a fair amount of time in my room for telling little white lies. My parents could always recognize when I was telling a "fib," as they put it, and would call me out on it constantly to curb this habit. The worst punishment was, without a doubt, when I would have to tell my friends that a story I had made up out of thin air was just that—a story.

My most outrageous lie in middle school had a good run. So good, in fact, that it stretched out for almost an entire school year. I don't know where the lie came from, but everyone in my class thought that I was best friends with the teenage tennis phenomenon Jennifer Capriati. As a teenager, Jennifer Capriati had captured the imagination of the nation. As she won tournament after tournament, I confided in my classmates one by one that we were best friends and pen pals. I told my friends that she would write long letters after each match and would come up with interesting tidbits that helped prove that we were great friends. After every major match, my friends would come to school on

Monday with a list of questions that I could posit to my famous pen pal. I have no idea why I decided to start this lie, where it came from, or why I felt so strongly about a friendship with someone I had never met, but this was my story and I was sticking to it. The more time that passed, the more elaborate the lie became. About a year into this particular lie, my mother overheard me telling my friends who were sleeping over that I had received a letter from my BFF Jennifer. My mother, having none of my pleading and swearing never to do it again, threw down the gauntlet, telling me, "You need to go tell your friends that it is not the truth." I am sure that the consequence was being grounded, so there was only one thing to do. Come clean.

I wanted to die. Seriously. It seems like the line between cool and uncool is so precarious in middle school. Now I was going to have to firebomb any chance of staying on the cool side by admitting that I was lying about the thing that made me cool in the first place? Awful. Despite my nonstop prayers between the conversation with my mom and the opening school bell on Monday morning, I was not kidnapped, nor did I have a freak accident that required emergency surgery and a long hospital stay. That Monday I went into class and told my friends that I did not, in fact, know Jennifer Capriati, and that actually I had been lying about our friendship the entire time. To their credit, they were kind to my face, but I felt like there was a level of suspicion that came with any of my previously unquestioned over-the-top tales for the next few years until I left for boarding school. Thank God my boarding school was in Connecticut, so that I was able to leave that lie far, far behind me.

Trust is hard to regain. I learned this lesson the hard way.

When you are selling anything in life, whether it be your

vision, your company, or yourself in a job interview, people need to believe that what you are telling them is true, and as the seller, you want to make sure that is the case. There will always be exceptions to the rule, but lead with the truth whenever you can to gain a reputation that you will be proud of in any crowd. As I discussed in earlier chapters, the key to selling is being able to effectively communicate your vision—a large part of that is selling yourself. If you are doing your job well, people believe that you are the authority on what you are selling because they believe you are at the top. The most important thing that you can do in the role of authority is tell the truth.

I have done sales coaching for some of the top fashion brands in the world, brands whose names epitomize the highest luxury that money can buy, like Armani and Fendi. Their clothes and accessories sell for thousands of dollars and their high-end items can sell for tens of thousands of dollars. One thing I tell their top salespeople time and time again is to be truthful when they are selling. When I am working with the sales teams, I ask them to picture this scenario. Let's say you work on commission, meaning that you get cash anytime you sell something in the store. Naturally, you are motivated to make a sale no matter what the consequence, right? Depends what your end goal is . . . and if you are working on commission, I suspect your end goal is money. Let's say that a very large woman comes in with a very large bank account to match. She is immediately drawn to an oversize coat made of feathers that costs an ungodly sum—thousands of dollars. You are working on commission, so naturally all you can think about is what you will do with your commission check. When the woman comes out wearing the coat and looking like a very large chicken, you turn on the charm and encourage her, despite knowing that she looks terrible, to purchase the coat. She listens to you, since you are the saleswoman of the year, and leaves with said coat wrapped and tied in a bow. You take your commission check and start clicking away on Net-a-Porter and hopefully putting some money into savings. Client gets her coat, you get the cash, everyone is happy, end of story. Or is it?

The problem with this scenario is that you were thinking about a quick sale, not the potential of a wealthy woman who hasn't figured out what looks best on her figure. While you are clicking away online, your wealthy client is going home to her husband or out to dinner with a friend who will probably tell her exactly what you did not—that the coat is awful and was a total waste of money. Your new client with money to burn will never burn her money with you again. She will probably tell a few friends to stay away from you as well. You made one good sale, but you could have made a client for life. If you had been honest up front and led her toward something less expensive that made her look great, she might have also bought something else to go with it that added up to more than the coat. Just because you weren't willing to tell her the truth doesn't mean that there won't be someone in her life who will—and someone is eventually going to tell her that she looks like Big Bird. It's just a matter of time. Remember this equation the next time you are tempted to sell something that doesn't live up to what you are hyping; if someone has a good experience with someone, they will mention it to one person; if they have a bad experience, they will mention it to nine people. In sales, you are only as good as your reputation. Don't ever put yourself in a situation where you put your reputation at risk.

I can tell you from experience what it is like to buy something that wasn't what it was cracked up to be. I had an incredibly talented woman sell me a four-day weekend at a lovely home in the Berkshires. She was the type of salesperson about whom people say to "stay away from tonight if you intend to have any money left in your wallet" before she goes onstage. She also does this signature move where she bangs down her gavel a few times before she starts an auction.

You might be able to guess who it was.

Moi.

I am so good at selling that I sold myself a four-day weekend to a house that I had never seen, in a place that I had never been, from a family I had never met.

And boy, was it a mistake. Another lesson learned. The hard way.

When I first started taking auctions, I was maniacal about ensuring that I was accurately portraying each item that I was selling before I went onstage. I would organize two or three calls with each nonprofit organization to go over their auction items in great detail, spend a couple of hours googling the lots so that I had a good sense of what I was describing, and in many instances spend at least an hour practicing everything before I went onstage. The more auctions I took, the more I realized that many supporters came back year after year. As a result, I would get feedback if people didn't have a good experience or weren't able to get something that I had promised them to drive up bidding in a heated bidding war. I learned to stay on script and made sure that I didn't embellish items for fear of getting the wrath of a client the following year. I didn't want to end up with a disappointed bidder or an angry supporter who felt that I had sold them a fake bill of goods. A large part of why these clients bid on lots at auctions is that they believe that if I am selling them something, they are getting the

Christie's stamp of approval. Certainly if I sold them something, it was the real deal. As I grew confident in my skills, my need for the multiple phone calls and hours of pre-event lot googling disappeared. I became less strict because I knew that I really could sell anything to anyone even if they slipped in a couple of extra lots right when I was walking onstage.

After a particularly long week of travel six years ago, I hosted an event with a relatively new organization that had organized their first-ever live auction only a week before the event. Because of my travel schedule, we had time for only one quick call before the big night. I received their list of five lots shortly before the auction that evening. As I waited in the wings to go onstage, the event organizer came up and handed me a couple of auction lots that she wanted to add. I glanced over the list quickly; the last lot they included was a four-day weekend stay at a house in the Berkshires in the summer.

The lot described a beautiful, renovated historic schoolhouse that boasted four bedrooms, a recently renovated kitchen, and a bubbling brook where you could swim if the weather was warm enough. My husband's birthday was coming up and I remember thinking that it would be a perfect surprise gift—I could invite three of our couple friends and we could celebrate his birthday at our big, beautiful house in the Berkshires next to the bubbling brook. Even if it was cold, we could all sit in front of the fireplace that I was certain the house would have and watch the Olympics. It would be absolutely perfect. I remember asking if there were any pictures of the house; there weren't, but since I was about to go onstage there was no time for a last-minute Google search. I jumped right into the auction as soon as I got onstage, and the auction moved along at a good clip until I came to the last auction lot. I introduced the lot and enthusiastically announced myself as the first bidder. After a minute of silence, one other bidder raised his hand, I quickly countered, and he didn't raise his hand again. I waited until it was obvious that no one else was going to bid, slammed down my gavel, and gave myself a mental high-five for scoring such an awesome gift for my husband at such a low price.

Flash-forward to a rainy Friday in June when I pull up to the aforementioned house in the Berkshires. My friend and I were both six months pregnant with our first children and had offered to drive up there early to ensure that everything was set by the time our other friends arrived. Her look of horror mirrored my own as I quickly realized that the reason that no one had bid on this "beautiful four-bedroom home in the Berkshires" was because the lot description was completely false, and clearly the audience was familiar with the donors of the house. Creepy collections of antique dolls, a pervasive smell of mold, a dampness that felt like it was on every couch and bed—the house felt like a set for a horror movie. If we'd had any cell service at the house, we probably would have called the other six people and told them to turn their cars around and head home. One after another, our friends arrived and I watched as their smiles quickly turned into wide-eyed despair at the thought that they would have to spend even a night in this house. The rain that pounded down the entire weekend didn't help, and even my hopes of watching the Olympics were dashed as we realized that there was only a twenty-one-inch TV with almost zero reception. I have never seen a group of people peel out of a house faster than we did on Sunday morning. The story still makes us all laugh to the point of sickness when talking about the weekend.

Lesson learned. The hardest way possible. In front of a group of friends who still bring it up at dinner parties.

I tell this story every year during my charity auctioneering classes to remind the candidates to research their lots before an auction. When you are selling an auction lot, a product, or a vision, remember that you are only as good as your word. Gaining a reputation as someone who will say anything to make a sale is a surefire way to firebomb your career before it even begins. Anytime you think about telling a lie to advance your sale, stop and think about the long-term ramifications for your career. Remember that your reputation is everything, and the Most Powerful Woman in the Room is known for her stellar reputation.

TWO OTHER POWERFUL WOMEN ON . . .

keeping their word

NINA GARCIA

Editor in Chief, *Elle* Magazine;
Project Runway Judge

In the fashion industry, many deals are made informally. A phone call with an old friend, coffee with a new colleague, or lunch to catch up with other industry leaders is often where promises are made and agreements put into place. And while such conversation might seem too casual to necessitate an obligation, I've learned that keeping up my end of any bargain is how to form concrete, lasting relationships. This logic works conversely as well; I never make a promise I know I can't keep. It can be tempting to tell potential business partners what they want to hear, but being up-front about expectations is key to maintaining integrity and credibility.

LINDA GUERRERO

Director of Latin America Publicity, Netflix

Life is a constant series of negotiations, especially for women. There's work; there's family; and there are the promises we make to ourselves. The entertainment industry can be particularly difficult terrain to navigate as agreements are all too casually made, broken, or changed without warning. In this profession, reputation is everything—it can open (or close) doors.

As much as I crave telling people what they want to hear in the moment, it's paramount for the health of my relationships in the long term to be honest up front. Before I give someone my word, I've learned to take a moment to consider what I'm capable of and what I'm willing to do—keeping in mind that whether it's business or personal, there's always room for negotiation.

THE MOST POWERFUL WOMAN IN THE ROOM . . .

12

exudes confidence

When I was working in the events department at Christie's, I was responsible for entertaining everyone from Valentino to President Clinton. My friends would always play it cool as we settled into postwork drinks, but you could be sure that after a few drinks the questions would start rapid-fire: What did he look like? Was he nice? Was he tall? What was she wearing? Did she really have an accent? What did they eat? What did they drink? At some point I would have to put an end to the questions because what I realized was that these people whom everyone obsessed over for hours at a time were all basically the same as you and me. Sure they were sipping Dom Pérignon at the Four Seasons hotel bar while I was heading downtown to meet my friends at a dive bar where champagne wasn't even on the menu, but the more time I spent talking to people I felt like I was supposed to be intimidated by, the more I realized that it actually was the same as talking to my friends. Well, my friends with more cash in the bank, better-applied makeup, a more expensive haircut, and better outfits.

When I first started out in special events in my twenties, there were many "is this really happening right now?" evenings. I spent an evening hanging out with Bono and his wife in our boardroom after he donated his paintings to a charity auction. I escorted Reese Witherspoon into the building one evening for a cocktail party. Leonardo DiCaprio held an auction at Christie's and my job was to ensure that a photographer captured a picture of him for the event. In each of those moments, I was a superfan—barely able to speak, bright red when spoken to, and incapable of acting like myself. These luminaries seemed as if they were in a different world, as out of reach as the CEO of my company. Surely they could see right through me and knew that my little black dress wasn't from Gucci. And my heels? They weren't exactly Chanel; I had picked them up at Loehmann's on the way to brunch with a friend the previous weekend. I knew from the magazines that these people were living in million-dollar mansions in the sky, whereas my apartment was also in the sky but I got there by walking up five flights of stairs. But what I have come to realize over the course of my career is that what drives every single one of the people is the same thing that drives anyone who reaches a high level of success in their career. They have found something that they love, something that they are good at doing, and have honed their craft with years of practice until they are the best in their field. They have had the same trials and tribulations that you and I have had—just on the world stage.

Fifteen years later, after many years spent practicing and perfecting my charity auction game, I am the person making the rules that everyone has to play by. Typically when a celebrity agrees to become the face of an organization, they join me onstage during the auction in order to drive up the bidding. Lydia as the auctioneer. Great! Lydia paired with Rihanna. Amazing!

But having a celebrity onstage is good only if we are working in tandem to drive up the bidding. Many of the celebrities I have worked with are movie stars who hate being put in a situation where they are off script, so they end up standing off to the side, as if they aren't even onstage. Other celebrities, like Seth Meyers, have no problem jumping into the role of co-auctioneer. In fact, we take so many auctions together that I refer to him as my "junior auctioneer trainee." That's right, late-night talk show host Seth Meyers is okay with being called a junior auctioneer trainee. How's that for humble? Not only does he not mind, but in our last auction together when I was all the way down at the other end of the stage about to sell a lot, he picked up my gavel and banged it down for me, exuberantly saying, "I think I'm getting the hang of this, Lydia." Most times I am paired with a celebrity, I find myself backstage in the minutes leading up to the auction in an almost laughable situation in which all of a sudden a world-famous celebrity like Hugh Jackman is peppering me with questions about the upcoming auction like one of my overserved friends at a dive bar would: What do I say? What do I do if no one bids? Should I tell a joke or be serious? Have you done this before? How can you do this all the time? Aren't you nervous? I have worked with everyone from Bruce Springsteen to Robert De Niro to Glenn Close to Whoopi Goldberg. Of course I'm nervous, but I'm the Most Powerful Woman in the Room, so I am going to embrace those nerves and rock the stage.

At these auctions, the people in the audience include titans of industry, best-dressed socialites, luminaries, and celebrities. The one thing I can tell you for sure is that although people may know that they are in positions of power or that they are famous, they do not think of themselves any differently than you think of yourself.

If someone has worked to achieve a certain degree of success in their industry—whether it be the CEO of a company, the head of a department, or the top player in their field—they deserve your respect. But if you are the Most Powerful Woman in the Room, you need to remember that being confident in yourself and your knowledge is what makes other people see you as powerful. In situations where I am backstage at Lincoln Center prepping for an auction with Hugh Jackman, I am the person in control of the conversation because I am the expert in my field. I am the expert in my field because I have put in thousands of hours ensuring that I am performing at the highest level possible.

I am sure you are reading this thinking, *As if I am ever going to be onstage with Hugh Jackman or Seth Meyers.* If you had asked me almost two decades ago if that would be a reality in my life, my answer probably would have been no. But that answer would have been for you; in my mind I would have been thinking that the answer was yes. I have been road-mapping my way to the top since I was little. I didn't know where my path would lead, but I knew, even growing up in a small town in Louisiana, that I had big dreams and that I wasn't going to stop until I fulfilled those dreams. You never know where your life will take you once you find your voice and the confidence to try anything. Put in the time and you will gain respect from your peers and from people you admire, because they will see themselves in you.

About ten years ago, I was asked to take an auction for a prestigious private school in Manhattan. This may seem odd to anyone who doesn't live in New York; however, many schools in the city hold an annual fundraising benefit gala. These are not your average affairs. Schools pull out all the stops, renting top event venues in the city, pulling together elaborate themes, and putting together truly one-of-a-kind auction lots. Think less of a classroom art project that the class created (which I have sold for thousands of dollars—for real) and more of a twenty-room ski chalet in Switzerland for a week or a private plane to an island that one of the parents owns. Teams of parents work for months in anticipation of the event; usually the most connected parents are responsible for pulling together the live auction lots. As there are a number of celebrities with children in private school in Manhattan, it goes without saying that there is usually an auction lot that includes something pulled together by that celebrity. I have auctioned off everything from the chance to sit in the front row at a basketball game with Ben Stiller to a dance lesson with Madonna to a lunch date with Robert De Niro, most of whom were sitting front row at the auction. These items can raise upwards of $20,000 at the school auctions. Many times the school will ask the celebrity if they would be willing to help during the auction, so I will end up with top chefs like Tom Colicchio or Marc Murphy onstage explaining what they are willing to offer and then helping me drive up the bidding. Each time one of the celebrities comes onstage with me, I am reminded that stars actually are just like us.

But even I, the person telling you about everyone putting their shoes on the same way in the morning, was still nervous after receiving a particularly exciting call from a school committee telling me that Matt Damon, a parent at the school, had agreed to come onstage during an upcoming auction. That's right. Jason Bourne and me. Onstage. Together.

I was a little nervous, since this was my first time with this particular school community; however, there was a silver lining to the event. The school had used a parent volunteer as their auctioneer for the past twenty-five years, so they had high hopes that I would be able to liven up their auction. Even the best auctioneer gets old playing to the same crowd year after year, so I was confident that it would be a good night. Additionally, I have seen enough interviews with Matt Damon to know that he has a good sense of humor, so I figured that not only would the crowd pay attention when he joined me onstage, but they might bid more if we were to work the crowd together. When the committee mentioned that he might join me onstage, I immediately suggested that he join me for the paddle raise. I knew that it would be more interesting to the audience to have him freshen up the event after a long live auction. If nothing else, having a world-famous celebrity onstage with me would make for a more interesting night than the ones they had previously witnessed. If, and only if, I didn't pass out.

Now, as you can imagine, every single person I have ever met knew that I was taking an auction with Matt Damon that evening. This was before Instagram, so it was truly boots-on-the-ground marketing on my part. But seriously, I had one chance to make sure everyone knew that this was about to happen, and I was not going to squander it. Even my jaded New York friends who pretend that they can't be bothered when I tell them about an experience that I found very cool or exciting showed rapt attention when I mentioned that I would be onstage with the cowriter and star of *Good Will Hunting*.

I nervously walked into Cipriani Wall Street the evening of the auction, dressed up and ready for the stage. Even the edifice of Cipriani Wall Street is imposing. It sits in the shadow of the New York Stock Exchange—a massive building with huge columns rising up from the street. As you walk through the revolving door, you are thrust into a cavernous room that looks like the inside of a building you might see in a movie set in Washington,

DC; a gorgeous old Greek Revival building with seventy-foot-tall ceilings and huge columns on all sides. As I arrived, the seven hundred perfectly dressed guests were slowly making their way to their tables. I timed my arrival near the end of cocktails, so that I could speak with anyone who needed to discuss last-minute additions before the auction. In this case, the event organizer grabbed my hand, and I followed behind her as she wove in and out of tables, careful not to step on the floor-length dresses of the women attending the event. I followed her through the crowd to my table, where she quickly found my place card a couple of seats away from Matt Damon. I thought that I would simply sit down at my seat and meet him later when he joined me onstage; however, the event organizer had other plans (which I believe included meeting Matt Damon herself). When she brought me over to meet him, I watched as she started to turn red and stammer, trying to find a word, any word, to come out of her mouth. As she turned to introduce me, I held out my hand and quickly introduced myself . . .

I will answer your questions in the order that they are coming to your brain:

1. Yes, he looks exactly like he does in the movies.
2. I did not scream, cry, or shriek, nor did I mention that I thought we should be best friends (though I really do feel that he would benefit from having me in his squad).

Even though inherently I know that Matt Damon is not actually Jason Bourne, I did feel like I needed to be on guard just in case something went south.

My husband has watched the Bourne trilogy no less than a hundred times, which means that I have probably seen it as many times. Naturally I felt like this would mean that Matt Damon would recognize me when we were introduced, even though I had never met him. He didn't know me. Obviously. We spoke briefly about the auction, and he agreed to come onstage for the paddle raise. I left quickly and returned to my seat.

After taking my place at the table, I didn't speak to him again for the rest of the dinner. I stood backstage mentally preparing for a long auction with a new crowd. As always, I started off the auction with my Strike and set the rapid, excitable clip that was going to be the auction for that evening. It was clear from the shocked look on the faces of the guests that this was going to be a markedly different evening from the ones they had attended in past years. Prices were climbing to five, ten times what the organizers had expected. The chairwomen of the event told me to be prepared for egregious talking throughout the evening; however, I found the opposite to be true. The audience was engaged, excited, and bidding like crazy. Lucky for me, one of my biggest bidding tables was the table where I had previously been seated. About halfway through the live auction, Matt and a few of the guys from my table got into a bidding war over one of the lots with a group from another table. The bidding kept climbing higher and higher and higher until we were well over double what the director of development had expected to make in her dream scenario. Matt and his seatmates were heckling me in a good-spirited way, and as we neared an astronomical amount for the lot, Matt yelled up at me.

"HEY, LINDSEY, LINDSEY—DOUBLE THE LOT."

There is always a person or two at an auction who can't help themselves. They may have attended an auction before or perhaps they fancy themselves the next great benefit auctioneer, or maybe they have just had too much to drink and want to be onstage.

Whatever the reason, the person decides to throw in well-meaning advice like "double the lot." In theory, it was a good idea, because when I double the lot, I push bidders up as high as they possibly can go before, in a surprise reveal, telling them that they both get the lot at the maximum price. However, in this case, I had only one lot to sell. Typically when someone from the audience tries to play the part of co-auctioneer, I will immediately make a joke to the effect of "Thank you for your helpful hints, sir, as I am sure you can imagine auctions work best when there is only one auctioneer doing the work." Acknowledge, thank them, remind them who is the Most Powerful Woman in the Room.

But what do you do when one of the world's biggest celebrities is (1) the person jumping in to offer advice, (2) calling you by the wrong name, and (3) about to join you onstage.

In that split second I knew that I had two choices: I could either treat the guy hollering from his seat like *People*'s Sexiest Man Alive and get busy changing my name to Lindsey, *or* I could treat him like any other parent at the school that night and make sure that he knew who was in charge.

Beyoncé calls her onstage personality Sasha Fierce—a way of describing the person that overtakes her normally shy persona when she is onstage in a glitter leotard OWNING the stage with razor-sharp dance moves and a serious set of pipes. Although I have yet to name my onstage persona (suggestions welcome), I understand how one side of your personality can become so strong that it refuses to let you back down even if your other side would let it slide. There is no question that my stage personality brings out the strongest, most confident side of myself. And that is the side of my personality that had no problem taking the comment head-on that evening,

"Sir, as you can imagine, I always like having a junior auction-eering assistant on hand in the crowd, but I can't double the lot because I only have one to sell."

Pause.

"And more importantly, my name is Lydia."

He let out a loud gasp followed by laughter, and I saw in the wide eyes of the other guests in the room that I had earned some serious respect for keeping my name. Following the insanely successful auction, Matt Damon came up onstage for the paddle-raise portion of the evening. As he strode onto the stage, he tried to make light of the early mistake by saying, "Hey, Lindsey." He turned to the audience and said, "This is just a joke that Lydia and I have—I just call her Lindsey." To which I replied to the audience, "The school did mention that there was a struggling actor who would be joining me onstage for the paddle raise, so let's give a round of applause for Mike Diamond." I don't know where the name came from or why I decided to rebrand Matt Damon as a struggling actor named Mike Diamond, but he was a great sport and played along for the rest of the auction. Many people came up to me afterward to marvel at my audacity. But come on, the Most Powerful Woman in the Room wasn't going to let that go. My name is, well, my name. Not going to change it. Even for Jason Bourne.

That night was a formative moment in my auctioneering career—if I held my ground that night, what could stop me? Since that auction many years ago, whenever I find myself in front of a room full of the world's wealthiest and most successful people, I don't even hesitate to stand my ground and treat them like equals. Anyone who has ever seen me onstage knows that I will squeeze every last dollar out of their wallet for the benefit of the organization that I am working for that evening. I have earned a great amount of respect by taking this skill and making it into something that translates to anyone, anywhere. I can't tell you how often I walk into a meeting in New York with a C-suite executive for one of the top institutions in the country and someone in the meeting will say, "Oh man, you got me to pay [insert ungodly sum of money] at the [fill in nonprofit's name] gala last week." They always say it with a laugh and a smile. No matter what type of person you encounter in your life journey, people will always respect someone who has mastered a skill that they do not possess. Whatever your passion leads you to in life, focus on excelling in that and remember to bring it to the table in a big way. The CEO of a company doesn't become the CEO by standing around letting other people take charge.

The interesting thing about formative moments like the one that I had onstage with Matt Damon is that I found that confidence spilling over into my day job as well. It is one thing to be dressed in a cocktail dress onstage rocking an auction, but what I enjoyed as much was feeling that same sense of empowerment in my job. This newfound attitude was part of the reason that I found myself walking up to the imposing HSBC Private Bank building in London on a bright, crisp September morning. Remember how I had pitched the idea of strategic partnerships to everyone in my company in order to make it happen? "The Collection of Elizabeth Taylor" had proven that my concept for strategic partnerships worked. But sales of that nature are few and far between—Christie's and Sotheby's compete ferociously to win the right to sell these landmark sales because it engages even the most difficult-to-reach collectors. The majority of our sales are made up of items from different collectors that do not have the added benefit of the world's first mega-celebrity attached to them. The notoriety and the public relations moments associated with a sale like "The Collection of Elizabeth Taylor" would be hard to replicate. As happens with every major project in the auction world, the day after a sale, everyone is already on to the next project looking for the next big auction piece or, hopefully, the next landmark collection. As the sale of Elizabeth Taylor's jewelry had occupied almost every minute of every day since I'd started strategic partnerships, it was now time to figure out what strategic partnerships would look like during a normal year in the auction world. I had a lot of downtime as well as a substantial hole in my budget that needed to be filled.

As I started pulling together my target lists, I decided that I needed to go straight to the top when making my requests. Everyone puts their shoes on the same way in the morning, right? I had been dealing with sponsorships long enough to know that decisions for big dollars were made at the top. I decided that the plan of attack was to stop reaching out to low and midlevel executives to forge the partnerships. It seemed like anytime I attempted to create a partnership with midlevel executives, things would get snared in red tape. In most companies if you can get the person who signs off on the check instead of the one who asks someone to sign the check, you soon realize that everyone below them is simply executing against their vision. Since I already had a decade plus on my résumé and the Christie's brand behind me, I was in a good position to make calls to people at any level. I knew that to unlock the kind of money I needed to bring in, I would have to begin at the top. I started reaching out to the most senior people in each company that I could find—cold-calling them, emailing their assistants—to see if anyone in the banking, hospitality, aviation, and automotive worlds would take a meeting.

If you are just starting out at a company, working at a start-up, or starting your own company, you may not be in a position to get to the top-level person on day one of your job, but you can always get to know the person who allows access to that person. Network with the people who have access to the person you ultimately want to get in front of so that you have someone else pulling for you as you advance in your career.

Spending time getting to know the assistant or person under the leader of a company is always a good idea because they could be the next person in line. If you are already treating them the way that the Most Powerful Woman in the Room treats her colleagues, it will be just a matter of time until you are sitting across from the person who is your ultimate target. There have been many times over my career that people on my team have asked me to meet with someone internally. I will make my own decision about someone, but a recommendation from one of my team members is about as good as it gets.

After a couple of weeks receiving polite but firm no-thank-yous from executive assistants, I received an exciting email from the chief marketing officer of Private Banking at HSBC, who was based in London, requesting a meeting. I could be there as soon as he had availability, I wrote back. He suggested the following Monday. Four days away. I didn't mention that I was based in New York, as I didn't want to give him the opportunity to suggest a call. I've said it before, and I will say it again. *Whenever possible, meet someone in person.* I recognize that you may not be in a role or a company that flies you to London for a meeting. When I first started working, no one was sending me to London for a meeting either. But if you do have the opportunity to meet someone face-to-face, maximize that opportunity and connect on a personal and professional level. Even if your meeting is all business, there will be a little downtime at some point that can be used to deepen your relationship. What do I mean by this? You need a point of connectivity that you can bring up the next time that you have a call or a chance to meet again. Sometimes it is the little things—where someone grew up, where they went to school, sports teams that they like, if they have children, a pet, anything that you can bring up again in subsequent conversations. If someone offers a chance to meet in their office, take the opportunity to look around to see if there are any points of connectivity. A family picture with kids always gives you the opportunity to ask about school breaks or vacation plans. Travel pictures are always a good way to ask about a place that you haven't been or a place that you have always wanted to go. Is someone a grandparent? Might as well put your feet up and have a drink, because you are going to be there a while if they start down that road. Pictures of pets can spark conversations about favorite types of dogs, cats, etc. Tell a quick story, relate on some level that makes a meeting more interesting than a simple transaction.

Back to London. Crisp morning. Imposing facade. HSBC. Newfound confidence. Or so I thought. As I walked up the stairs and through the large front door, I could feel my nerves getting the best of me. *What if I threw away a job that I knew how to do like the back of my hand to do something that doesn't work out? What if strategic partnerships isn't going to work and I am going to be out of a job in a month?* It doesn't matter how much self-confidence you have; when you are really putting yourself out there, it is easy to start to doubt yourself. But those are the moments when you have to dig deep and believe in yourself, believe that the time you have invested in getting to the top of your game will pay off, and try to exude confidence. Remember that a good poker face will get you far in life. Even if on the inside you are shaking, keep a cool, calm exterior and press on. After giving my name to the front counter, accepting their offer of a cup of tea, and walking into a massive room with huge windows overlooking the street, I settled into a chair and began to review my pitch in my mind. I rehearsed my carefully prepared opening statement so that I could launch right into my pitch without hesitation. A Strike without a gavel. A few short minutes later, a young woman arrived to take me up to the office of the global head of marketing and communications. I was pleasantly surprised, and a little relieved, when I walked into an office that was smaller than my office in New York and was asked to wait for a few minutes, as he was running late for the meeting. I spent the next couple of minutes looking around his office, familiarizing myself with his life—children, travel pictures, awards and degrees bestowed upon him from various jobs and universities. By the time he arrived, I felt like I already knew the guy. Armed with this information, I found that the gentleman in front of me was no longer an imposing force behind one of the greatest marketing campaigns of that decade; he was a guy with a family who liked to travel and was good at his job.

I started off by asking about his role at HSBC and the partnerships that he felt were successful for the firm. As he delved deeper into his history of partnerships within the firm, I saw a natural transition and used it to launch my pitch at a rapid clip, explaining strategic partnerships, talking about what made it different from other programs in the marketplace, and mapping out the number of cities globally where our companies could activate programs. At this point there was a natural transition from our discussion about countries where Christie's and HSBC were located into a conversation about travel . . . his favorite travel destinations, my favorite travel destinations, and finally back to strategic partnerships. I had prepared a hardcover book outlining the program, and he paged through it thoughtfully, remarking about particular things, asking questions as they came to him, and then giving me tips about where to travel in a country I expressed interest in visiting that year. It was my favorite type of pitch—professional but also personal—and the kind where I walk away feeling like I have effectively communicated my pitch but also gotten to know the person on the other side of the table as more than a person I am connected to on LinkedIn.

I left the office feeling confident that I would hear from him again. I was right. It was four months later, a week before I left work for my wedding and honeymoon, that I received a call saying that he wanted a formal proposal about everything that we had discussed in our meeting. I worked tirelessly with my colleague to come up with as close to a finished proposal as possible before I left for my wedding. When I arrived at my hotel in Tahiti, I found the final proposal from my office awaiting last-minute edits sitting on the table that looked out onto an endless world of turquoise blue. I picked it up and tossed it in the trash. You get only one honeymoon—who wants to spend it editing a proposal? Even the Most Powerful Woman in the Room needs to recharge.

I sent the final proposal the day after I returned to the office from my honeymoon, and a week later he called to tell me that they would be signing on for a strategic partnership. A thrilling call on every level, but perhaps even more so because I genuinely enjoyed working with the person on the other end. After we signed the agreement, every time I was in London for work I made a point to stop by his office for our meetings, instead of slotting it into one of the many calls I had to make that day. When he decided to move on from HSBC, he stopped by Christie's in London to have a cup of tea with me to inform me of his departure and tell me all about his new plan. It was a pleasure to find a human connection with someone I worked with over the course of many years, chief marketing officer or not.

The Most Powerful Woman in the Room understands that no matter how high someone ascends into the ranks of their job or in the stratospheres of celebrity, they are still looking to connect through shared emotional experiences and will always respect someone who has put in the time to rise to the top of their game. The Most Powerful Woman in the Room is not intimidated by power but instead seeks out others who have gained respect and power with hard work and a persistence that has led them to the top of their field. She seeks their advice and their counsel, and she road-maps her life so that ultimately people will be seeking her advice and counsel as the Most Powerful Woman in the Room.

when they knew they had made it

ALEXANDRA BUCKLEY VORIS

Cofounder, Bitsy's Brainfood

Rather than wasting a bunch of energy trying to morph into someone she's not, a powerful woman knows that when she grabs hold of her straight-up self, without apologizing for what she thinks she lacks or getting angsty about who she isn't—when a woman doesn't just "accept" herself but rather says, *This is who I am*—that is when power is seized. The minute I started to understand not only that my sensitivity wasn't a weakness but also that it's at the heart of what makes me strong, that was when everything changed.

MARY GIULIANI

Author, Lifestyle Expert, and Celebrity Caterer

Very early in my career, I received a call from the world's finest event planner Colin Cowie's office that he wanted me to cater an event for Elizabeth Taylor with *InStyle* at Christie's. Those are four very fancy names in one sentence.

However, if Liz's signature color was violet, mine was green, because that is exactly what I was. Novice doesn't even come close. It had been only two months since I started my job as catering sales representative at DM Cuisine. I barely knew the difference between a salad fork and an entrée fork, but a moment revealed itself to me in this opportunity; it was up to me and me alone to figure out what to do with it.

When I opened the boardroom doors at Christie's, I could not believe what I was seeing. The room was filled with top-level Christie's executives, the whole executive team from *InStyle*, and a team of Elizabeth Taylor's most trusted handlers. I looked around and just observed this room filled with accomplished high-level executives, my heart racing with that "Please don't call on me, please don't call on me" feeling.

When lavender carpets, crystals, elephants (yes, elephants), Nehru jackets for the men responsible for picking up the elephant poop, lighting, sound, press, and VIP guests were checked off, it was my turn to present my menu ideas. I began to rattle off a list of very fancy food items that I barely knew how to pronounce. Colin also chimed in with even fancier suggestions, things like caviar and chervil.

Quickly we were stopped by Elizabeth Taylor's team, who informed us that Liz did not like fancy foods and to stop with all the caviar and Chilean sea bass talk. As long as there were pigs in a blanket and mini cheeseburgers at the party, she would be happy. This news delighted me, as those were my two favorite foods on the planet.

I realized in that moment that if I was going to have a career in food catering to the finest names in the biz, then I was to be honest and genuine about the foods I love to cook and serve. Authentic, down to earth, approachable was what I was. I didn't have a fancy or pretentious bone in my entire body, so why would I serve foods that were? Two years later, I started my own business, and guess what our number one seller for the past thirteen years has been? Tiny hot dogs.

BETTINA PRENTICE

Founder and Creative Director, Prentice Cultural Communications

Eighteen years ago, I started out at the front desk of Sotheby's. Most of the people who walked through the doors treated me as if I were invisible; others were polite. On the worst days, I would have to sit stoically while some hotshot shouted at me or pointed a finger in my face because the person they wanted to see was out of the country or not available. Starting at the bottom taught me a lot about dignity, respect, empathy, and grace under pressure.

For everyone starting out, the experience will give you the tools that you need to navigate difficult situations, and you are guaranteed to treat those around you with respect for the rest of your career. I now own a cultural communications agency with an enviable client list and am proud that we have a supportive, gracious environment where hard work is celebrated and talent is nurtured. Whenever I am in the final stages of hiring for a new position, I share my own front-desk experience with candidates. I believe that life is a meritocracy. Today's assistant editor is tomorrow's editor in chief.

THE MOST
POWERFUL
WOMAN
IN THE
ROOM . . .

13

inspires others and leads by example

"Stay in your lane" was a phrase that I heard throughout my career. I overheard it as I walked through the office from men and women, young and old. I heard people use it on conference calls, on television during interviews, in meetings, and with friends at dinner. Like most phrases that become part of the everyday lexicon of people in the working world, it is a perfect sound bite: digestible, and easy to visualize.

NEWSFLASH: The Most Powerful Woman in the Room will not be staying in her lane.

There is no question that there are times when it makes sense to stay in your lane; in most cases it has to do with getting your job done. But there is a world of possibility out there, and if you stay in your lane, you will never give yourself the chance to be open to all the other incredible things that you could be doing.

I host a quarterly networking breakfast with a woman who, at one time, was one of my biggest rivals in the auction world. "Rival" is a strong word, especially for someone you have never met.

But when I was in my twenties, I truly believed that Courtney Smith, who held the same position as mine at Sotheby's, our biggest competitor in the auction world, was as interested in what I was doing in my job as she was doing in her own. In my twenties, I had a lot more time than I do today to think about, worry about, and create a dramatic story line that didn't exist. Flash-forward over a decade later, with three small children running around, a full-time job running a department by day and auctions at night, and I not only don't know anything about my contemporary at Sotheby's, but I don't have time to care. Nor do I have the inclination to create a story line about anything except getting home and getting more than five hours of sleep.

In my early working years, however, all I knew was that Courtney Smith was running the events department at Sotheby's, and that made us rivals. Anytime a client slipped up and mentioned they had attended a fabulous event at Sotheby's, a small part of me would become exceedingly jealous at the thought that they were doing things better than I was. Whenever an article came out about a lavish affair at Sotheby's, I pored over it to ensure they weren't thinking of anything I hadn't thought of first. Courtney Smith was the Pepsi to my Coke, the Apple to my Samsung. Ten years of doing the exact same job at the world's two largest auction houses. It took, of all things, a charity auction in California to bring us together.

I arrived at a stunning estate set on the shore of Lake Tahoe for the pre-event cocktail reception for the Save Lake Tahoe auction and Oscar de la Renta fashion show. It was my first time there, and I relished the picture-perfect wide blue sky of a Northern California night, a chill settling into the air as the sun began to set. As is often the case at a pre-auction cocktail reception in a different city,

I rarely know anyone at the event. But as you may have guessed by now, I see this as a blank slate of opportunity. Network or Die, remember? In a situation like this, my goal is to meet as many people as possible so that by the time I go onstage the next day, I have formed quick friendships with people who don't mind if I call on them to start my bidding or quiet the room. Part of being an effective auctioneer or in business is making people feel like you are part of their community. I spend a lot of time reviewing the notes, ensuring that I am using the right acronym to describe their organization, and becoming friendly with the auction chairs in hopes that they will lend me a raised hand if the auction starts to stall. On more than one occasion, my top bidder has been someone I befriended the night before the auction, who enjoys the benefit of a few minutes of extra attention in a crowd of 500 people.

I usually spend the first few minutes after I arrive surveying the room to figure out if I recognize any of our clients, or praying that there is a familiar face or two among the crowd. At the Lake Tahoe event, after glancing furtively around, I realized I didn't know anyone, so I decided to make my way outside to the expansive lawn to see if I had better luck there. As I approached the door, I saw a woman walking directly toward me. There is also an odd side effect of spending time onstage in front of hundreds of people seventy to a hundred times a year. I get stopped by people who strike up a conversation with me as if we know each other before we have even met. I get stopped at the park, on the street, at dinner, and on the beach by people who think we are friends. Whenever someone starts a conversation with "You look so familiar," if they don't look familiar to me, my first question is "Have you been to an auction recently?" By the huge smile on her face, I assumed that she was one of the people who had seen me onstage and now thought I was her sister's best friend or her yoga teacher (I wish). However, as she came closer and closer, I noticed something oddly familiar about her. As she walked up to me, she gave me a huge smile and said, simply,

"Lydia, I'm Courtney Smith."

Even on the other side of the country in a remote place where her name shouldn't have meant anything to me, it certainly meant something. We hugged like old friends, spent the next two hours of the cocktail reception ignoring everyone else while we recounted stories of our early years in the auction world, and ended up going to a nearby restaurant that evening for a four-hour dinner. The conversation was meandering at best—we covered everything from our personal lives to our professional lives to war stories from our time in the events department and the auction world. It was so amazing to spend time with another woman who had been through the exact same experiences in her twenties. Unlike yours truly, Courtney had moved on to work at one of the top jewelers in the world, Graff Diamonds, which made it much easier to have a real conversation about our experiences. She was in charge of marketing and events, and Graff was sponsoring the Save Lake Tahoe auction, which I would be taking the next day. Her career was on fire because of her hard work and ingenuity—her next move would come shortly after we connected: starting a new division called Private Client Services at Fendi. I told her how I devised strategic partnerships and was now solely focused on creating large-scale partnerships for Christie's around the world. After that long dinner covering everything we could think of, we parted ways for the evening. We saw each other briefly the next day prior to the auction and exchanged a quick hello, but following the auction we were back together covering everything that we had forgotten to discuss the night before. After returning to New York, we stayed in touch and began to meet for dinner semi-regularly.

One night over dinner at Hudson Clearwater, a cozy West Village restaurant with a back patio that makes you feel like you are sitting in a tiny backyard in the middle of New York City, Courtney and I found ourselves in the middle of a conversation that went a little bit like this:

Me: ". . . and then I was having a meeting with my amazing friend Mary—you know Mary, right?"

Courtney: "No. But that reminds me—I wanted to talk to you about meeting with Ashley. You have met her before, right?"

Me: "No."

After the third time this happened over the course of dinner, we both paused for a second and then agreed almost instantaneously that we needed to start a networking SOMETHING. We thought about doing cocktails, but that didn't seem quite serious enough. And a lunch seemed too easy to flake on when meetings started getting in the way or kids needed to be picked up/dropped off from school. So we settled on a breakfast—before anything could get in the way of the day. Who doesn't like to start their morning with inspiration and a big cup of coffee? We would both invite friends whom the other hadn't met and our friends would benefit from meeting other friends whom we considered incredible, capable, and amazing. Hence, the networking breakfast began.

In the years leading up to this moment with Courtney, I had been lucky enough to receive an annual invitation to the "Ladies Who Don't Lunch" lunch every year right before Christmas in the private wine cellar of the 21 Club. Hosted by the formidable Alexandra Lebenthal, dubbed the "Queen of Wall Street" by *Fortune* magazine, it was my first invitation into the world of big-league power women. The 21 Club wine cellar dinner is the epitome of old-world New York. When you walk down the steps past the iron gates with painted jockeys atop each post, you immediately feel like you have been swept back into a different era. After checking your coat, you follow the maître d' through the bustling restaurant, filled with buzzed patrons celebrating amid the holiday decorations, and through the kitchen, where one of the waiters dressed in black tie rings a bell to let everyone know that you are coming through. After navigating the slippery floor and dodging waiters with trays of food, you walk down a flight of stairs into the basement, where they lead you to a door that is part of a wall and must be at least four feet thick. After ducking under a few pipes while holding on to shelves stacked with wine racks, you find yourself semi climbing through an *Alice in Wonderland*–style hole in the wall to reveal a wine cellar that doubled as a dining room during Prohibition.

The table seats only twenty-two, though upon occasion Alex has charmed them into seating twenty-four. You can almost feel the memories of a bygone era as you sink into the comfortable club chairs for lunch in the tight quarters surrounded by bottles of wine. You think time disappears when you are in a casino? Try the 21 Club's wine cellar. Sometimes when I leave to "go back to work" after that lunch, I am not sure I could even tell you if I was leaving on the same day that I arrived. It is a quintessential New York power room, and Alex invites an impressive roster of New York City women to join her for lunch each December. Without a doubt the most memorable part of the lunch for me has always been the question that she poses to the group—a personal question that everyone around the table has to answer, but one that is also something unexpected, like "What was your first concert?"

You learn so much about a person by the way they tell a story, and this lunch has been an incredible moment to bear witness to women at the highest levels of finance, fashion, media, and beauty share how they became who they are today. It has been amazing to return to that special place once a year in this iconic New York landmark and listen to women whom I admire and respect reflect on their lives and their careers.

It was with Alex's lunch in mind that I suggested to Courtney we follow a similar format at our networking breakfast. On the morning of our first networking breakfast, Courtney and I arrived early and anxiously awaited our first guests at a small restaurant in the West Village. The guest list was composed of twelve people; each of us had invited five people whom the other person did not know, and introductions were made as everyone arrived. After letting everyone get comfortable with their seated tablemates, I quieted everyone down and thanked them for coming. Courtney and I posed a simple request to the group: "Tell us what is going on in your life." As I mention in my chapter on public speaking, it is amazing to watch even the most confident women get a little uncomfortable when asked to speak in front of a group of people they don't know. Especially when asked to answer a personal question. Everyone sat staring at us for a little bit, shifting nervously in their chairs, and then one of the women volunteered to speak. That first vote of confidence was all the breakfast really needed to take off; one by one, the women answered the question and then kept going.

As often happens with groups of women, within minutes the conversation took on a life of its own. We had assumed that a networking breakfast would largely focus on careers and questions about people's jobs in general. It became clear very quickly that no one was going to address their career path without talking about their personal lives as well. In some cases, there was no career at all—they were just there to meet new people and share.

And share they did. About everything. And the more people shared, the more they got in return. I had assumed that the breakfast would take roughly an hour and had blocked off time in my calendar accordingly. Two hours into the breakfast, I finally had to pull the plug—no one wanted to leave. As we sat in a taxi on the way uptown to our offices, Courtney and I couldn't stop recounting what had just happened. You always hear stories of women wanting to tear each other down instead of build each other up. This could not have been further from what we had experienced. It was as if the twelve people around the table were each bringing different perspectives and viewpoints that were interchangeable and additive to everyone else around the table. It was like having a group of cheerleaders who were acknowledging the work that you had done as a career woman, as a mom, as a woman doing it on her own, as someone just starting her own business and celebrating her success. As twelve individuals with nothing but two people in common, we were all drawn to the idea of helping one another. The breakfast that had started off with ten strangers and two points of contact had become a new network for all of us.

We quickly realized that we were on to something when a few weeks later we started getting emails from our friends asking when we were planning to hold the next breakfast. The next question was "Is it okay if I invite my friend/my colleague/someone I met who is in a rut?" The breakfast quickly became like a drug—a group of women, many of whom had never met, supporting issues in one another's personal life and professional life, and opening up their networks to lift everyone up. Over the four years that we have held the breakfast, what started as a group of twelve women has turned into a breakfast that has touched over a hundred women. It has grown from twelve people to as large as twenty-five people. It is a place where we invite anyone in need of life guidance, career guidance, a fresh take on a new business, a place to talk about breakups, babies, divorce, motherhood, the challenges of marriage, fertility issues, career changes, career success—you name it, we have covered it. We ask everyone at the table the same question: "What are you working on?" Because, as you know, a powerful woman always has her sights set on something, whether it's starting a business, raising a family, running the PTA, or creating a new strategy for fundraising on behalf of a nonprofit.

As Courtney and I cross paths with people in our own lives who need a different perspective or a fresh take on personal or business issues, we invite them to join us. People who attend the breakfast are also welcome to suggest people they feel would benefit from the advice of those around the table. Even the demographic of women has shifted; whereas it used to be women in their mid-thirties, it now includes women from their mid-twenties to their late forties, all sharing life advice and different perspectives on the ever-changing and challenging world that we live in. It is open to any woman who expresses a need for a change or an interest in starting a new chapter within her professional and personal lives. Some people attend every networking breakfast; some people miss two and come back; some never come back, constrained by time or energy. The beauty of the networking breakfast is the combination of new and returning attendees. The new attendees bring new life and new energy to the mix, as well as different topics of conversation; people who have come time and time again update us on what is taking place in their lives. The breakfast serves as a place where people come to share exciting news; in my case, I couldn't wait to tell everyone when I sold this book. I had spoken about the book for years, and when I finally finished the proposal and sold it a couple of weeks later, the reaction from the attendees was overwhelming enthusiasm followed by offers to host book signings or set up speaking engagements. One of our attendees shared her fertility struggles and then a year later brought her newborn to the breakfast. Another shared marital woes and then returned to a breakfast almost a year later to announce that they had worked through their issues. Women starting businesses come for advice from other women who have already done it. Full-time moms looking to get back into the working world come to network for new opportunities and possibilities. All of them express a want for something new, a new way to look at something, advice from women who have gone before them or their peers, or the chance to share something that they learned the hard way.

The women coming to the breakfasts who are in their twenties have inspired me—they look at work as one of many different possibilities in life. They don't feel as if work is something that should own you, but it should be fulfilling and creative. The women in their twenties also bring a fresh perspective and lack of fear about upsetting what many of those in our thirties and forties perceive to be cultural norms. One woman who works at a prominent luxury brand mentioned that she had given up her apartment and was living solely off accommodations on Airbnb for a year as a way to save money and try out living in different neighborhoods in NYC. In a city where living in the right area and getting your kid into the right school are talking points among a lot of my peers, it was refreshing to hear her announce this without any embarrassment or fear of judgment. Other women in their twenties had the same reaction that I had when learning about life as an Airbnb-er when I told them that I was entering my twentieth year at Christie's. Not one other person at the breakfast that day was still at the company where they began their career. In addition, they seem unconcerned with gaps on their résumé after bouncing from company to company.

I am constantly encouraging my peers in their thirties and forties to look behind them at the next generation and understand how beneficial their thinking is to their goals. They don't see roadblocks; they see limitless potential. Encourage them, get to know them—their openness to experience and life is fantastic. It will challenge the way you see life and maybe even encourage you to get a side hustle. In many ways, if you are a decade or two out of college, you have already spent the time mastering your skills, so now is the time to diversify those skills. And just as we can learn from women in their twenties, they can learn from women in their thirties and forties. Many of the women attending the breakfast in my peer group have also reached a level of success either in their own business or in the company that they have been working in for years, or they have been out of work for years and created a completely new skill set juggling the schedule of children as a full-time mom. They are ready for something new, ready for a next step, but also have responsibilities that can't be ignored, like children, school tuition, aging parents. They have either worked in a company for a long time and are looking to make a change, have hit a point in their entrepreneurial career where they have a ton of experience, or have had children and are trying to figure out how to make it all work together. Every age group brings a different perspective to the table.

For me the breakfast has been an absolute blast. I love spending time with my peers as much as I love spending time with women in their twenties, because I am an entrepreneur at the core. Though I have been with my company for twenty years, I had to create something new to stay. Even now, when my days are already insanely busy, I am always looking for another opportunity to seek out new information or try something new. I was in love with the idea of a side hustle before people started wearing the phrase on T-shirts. Being able to share my thoughts on the topic and hear the thoughts of other women who are single, engaged, married, full-time moms, working moms has been invaluable—we all have advice to share with others around us. For me, it is the opportunity to draw from past experiences and help others who might be seeking advice at any point in their career.

Whatever stage you are at in your life, think about putting together a moment for this type of connection. Even if you start it on your own and you are the only point of connection between the people at the table, you can create this for those around you. In many ways, it is about flipping your mind-set; when you start seeing other women as an additive piece of your networking puzzle, you will be amazed at how helpful your advice can quickly become to those around you. When speaking to college seniors requesting advice on how to move into the working world, I always recommend that they reach out to women two or three years out of college. I can remember that transitory time, but who better to give guidance than someone who has recently passed through that stage in their life. Same with women who are looking to transition jobs, having their first child, or going back to work after their first child. Talking to someone who has already been in the trenches of a life experience and has found their way to the other side can be hugely helpful when you are just going through it.

I find that the networking breakfast buzz lasts for days. Very few things in life will get you further than a loyal group of women who are supportive of you because you are supportive of them. Women talk. Let's strip out the negativity and the talk that rips people down, and instead use that talk to build people up. The message you should be putting out there about yourself is that you are inclusive, positive, and ready to help others succeed in their life. The more you say it, the more you will start to live it.

My biggest takeaway from the networking breakfast? For those of you who are thinking that getting out of your lane is impossible, that you will be successful only by doing exactly what you are told, let me dispel you of that notion. I have been seated at a breakfast table with women who for the past four years have done the opposite and continue to excel in their lives. We do not live in a world defined by borders anymore. Information is available to anyone at any time. You will need to get a job to pay for your life—yes, that's real life. But you can also find things on the side that allow you to explore your passion, which can be monetized and isn't fulfilled when you are sitting behind a computer in a windowless office. Work is no longer about going to an office where you grind at the same thing day in and day out. Work is a place where you learn the skills that you can apply to other things that interest you. You can spend your days working at a job that pays the rent and then use any additional time to work on something that you are truly passionate about. In a perfect world, that skill becomes something that you can monetize enough to pay the rent and fund all your dreams along the way. Even if it doesn't become something that you can monetize, adding an additional dimension to your life helps you think in a new and different way about things that can become mundane and repetitive.

We are not wedded to the past, where we each chose a lane and stayed in it. We are living in the future, where we can build our own communities without lanes, where the value in networks cannot be understated. It is so easy to put your head down and grind away either in life or in work, to never stop to look around and realize that you are the only person who can change the path that you are on. Stop putting your head down; look up and reach out. Find like-minded people and connect with them. Start your own networking breakfast, coffee break, or cocktail hour and start thinking outside the box. Be open to trying something new, and if it doesn't work, try something else.

The Most Powerful Woman in the Room is an information seeker, a connector of people, and she is constantly listening to the advice of other women in her life. Sometimes all she needs is a forum to share her ideas and learn from others. So be the one who steps forward and invites everyone into a place where support and encouragement are the name of the game.

My question to you, the Most Powerful Woman in the Room, is: When is your breakfast?

TWO OTHER POWERFUL WOMEN ON . . .

inspiring others

SARAH KATE ELLIS

CEO, GLAAD

I have always understood the power of stories, including my own, and their singular capacity to change the world. Stories are the way we understand society, how we learn, and how we grow in our acceptance of people and ideas. Witnessing the power of sharing my story of simultaneous pregnancies and navigating the road to motherhood with my wife led me to shift from helming some of the most respected and successful magazines to running GLAAD, the world's largest LGBTQ media advocacy organization. Every day, I make sure other people's stories are told in the same authentic, respectful, and beautiful way that I was able to share my family's story with the world. I lead by example, and now both shape and anticipate the diverse and inspiring narratives that change society. You will inherit whatever society you help create, so make sure it is one that you are proud of.

COURTNEY SMITH

Vice President,
Private Client Relations & Events, Fendi

Community is a cornerstone in every aspect of my life—and the life I have been creating with my daughter. A core value I find driving decisions daily. I strive to ensure my daughter feels this sense of family and community (our loved ones are often far away) with the people who we choose to have around us.

I am extremely fortunate to have many incredible women in my life who continue to inspire me every day. I have always believed there is no greater gift to each of them than to connect them with one another. Creating an authentic, supportive, empowering community to thank these remarkable ladies and watch amazing ideas and synergies take flight has been a privilege. And the power of community: invaluable.

THE MOST POWERFUL WOMAN

IN THE ROOM IS YOU

When I signed my book deal and the publisher asked, "How quickly can you write it?" I took a second. First-time author, three kids (the youngest only eight months old at the time), full-time career, second job at night . . .

"How quickly do you need it?"

I am writing this final note sitting on a plane en route to an auction in San Diego, where I will be for exactly twenty hours so that I can catch an early flight tomorrow to be home to put the kids to bed.

I woke up at 4:00 this morning, nursed my daughter at 5:00 a.m. and hailed a cab while mentally ticking off my ever-growing to-do list, and was in line for a large skim latte at JFK by 7:00 a.m.

I should be exhausted.

I am elated.

A roadblock that seemed insurmountable hurdled.

A box next to a major life goal on my road map checked.

Although I have written every word of this book, the energy and the encouragement that I needed to make this happen came from my community. Every breakfast, lunch, dinner, cocktail, walk, run, and moment spent with my family, friends, and the incredible women in my life has fueled and inspired me. Friends I haven't spoken to in years, colleagues I worked with years ago, and people I barely know have reached out to encourage and cheer me on every step of the way. The minute I posted the news on social media that I sold my book, I knew I could do it. I had to do it. There was no alternative. My community would never have let me fail.

When I think back to the beginning of my journey in New York, to the twenty-one-year-old woman lugging a suitcase up the stairs to a new life and a new future, I am so thankful for the trials and tribulations that brought me to this place. Each life moment that I have revisited over the course of this book has affirmed what I already knew: to be the Most Powerful Woman in the Room takes work, dedication, and the desire to set goals higher and higher. We can't do it alone and we shouldn't want to do it alone. There are so many people out there who are letting life pass them by because they are stuck in a rut or unsure of their next step. Use your vision and your leadership, and bring them along with you. The Most Powerful Woman in the Room knows how to command an audience and sell her way to success. The success that she wants to see in her life, and the lives of those around her.

Let the last page of this book be the start of a new journey for you. A journey where you know that you can attain anything that you set your mind to in life.

As I said at the beginning of this book, the Most Powerful Woman in the Room is me.

But now, the Most Powerful Woman in the Room is you too.

Acknowledgments

My greatest gift in life is the abundance of family and friends that make up my world. This book would not have been possible without their love and support.

I begin where I began. Mom and Dad, thank you for giving me life. In every childhood memory I can see your faces on the sidelines supporting, encouraging, offering advice, hugs and kisses. From Bobcat soccer games to volleyball games to ballet recitals to auctions, you have always been front and center cheering louder than anyone else. Your loves and interests have shaped me into who I am today.

Mom—your love of travel, adventure, fashion, and your incredible people skills have shown me how exciting life can be if you keep your eyes open to new possibilities.

Dad—your love of reading, conversation, and networking have taught me to live a life filled with curiosity and to always be a lifelong learner. Together you taught me the most important life lesson of all: Never Give Up.

Thank you for being such wonderful parents and extraordinary grandparents to Beatrice, Henry, and Eloise.

I love you both so much.

To my husband, Chris, who encouraged me every step of the way, making dinner for me as I wrote late into the evening, bringing me flowers when I finished drafts, and whisking the kids away on an adventure whenever I had an inspired thought and needed a moment of quiet to write. Thank you for giving me the time and support I needed to make this book happen. I love you.

To Beatrice, Henry, and Eloise, there are no words to describe my love for you. I have loved each of you since the minute that I met you. My fondest memories of this writing process all have to do with you: Beatrice curled up next to me on the couch writing her book, Henry coming in repeatedly to give me kisses when he knew he was supposed to stay out so I could write, and Eloise peeking her sweet little face in the room every few minutes to simply say "Mama." The greatest word in the English language spoken differently by each one of you. I could spend the rest of my life kissing your little faces. I hope that you will grow to be strong, intelligent, kind citizens of the world, and I will be here to support you every step of the way.

When I look at my children, I see the faces and personalities of my siblings. I am truly the luckiest sister in the world to be blessed with three strong, independent, funny, charming, and interesting siblings. Charles, you have always been such a kind, caring older brother. Thank you for always looking out for me, and always supporting me in life. Andrew, you have always been such a strong, smart, talented brother. It has been so amazing to watch you excel in your career, your athletics, and your friendships. Hilary, you are the best sister I could have ever asked for in life. You are an amazing aunt, a true friend, and one of the funniest people I know. There are few things I love more than sitting next to you while you laugh. Thank you too for never giving up shotgun even when I was the clear winner; you taught me that even if you win, you might still need to try a little harder. I love you guys.

To Steve and Beth for your incredible love and generosity.

Thank you for treating me like one of your own children, loving my children, and providing such incredible support for our family. I am blessed to have you in my life. Katelyn, thank you for being a wonderful sister-in-law. Sue Garvey, you are so thoughtful and kind.

My childhood memories are filled with so many wonderful trips to the English countryside and visits to London. I will forever love scones, clotted cream, and strawberry jam thanks to summers spent with my hilarious aunts and uncles, Sue, Mary, Julia, Big Andrew, and Bean. And so much love goes to my English cousins, Stuart, Alice, Emily, Oliver, Bertie, Ben, and Hugo.

Friendships can be made at any point in life, but my oldest friend, Corinne: your ability to see the positive in anyone is what makes you truly one in a million. I am the luckiest woman in the world to have grown up with your friendship, kind soul, and infinite patience.

To Mary Lucille. The only person I have ever met with dreams as big as mine. This is our year. Or perhaps it has always been our year. I am so blessed to have a friend who has given me unwavering support through every up and down. This book would never have happened without your friendship, guidance, and support. I can't wait to dream up our next adventure.

When I drove up the mountain through the gates of Sewanee, I had no way of knowing that the friendships I would make in those four years would be the most incredible friendships of my life. Lina—from the first days in our tapestry-covered room in Gorgas to our midnight runs to the Cross all the way to Compass Point in Antigua, your friendship has been such a gift in my life. Auburn—thank you for making my business trips to San Fran feel like I am visiting my second home, for providing free makeup lessons, and for being the best travel partner a girl could ask for. I can't wait for India. To Sarah, Little Tyke, my partner in hanging out of the sunroof—looking forward to many more years of glasses of wine on the beach in Boca Grande. Scottie—my birthday twin. Time never passes between us. Thank you for letting me be Flynn's godmother, and for your love and friendship all these years. Brooksie—from our first meeting at Merestead to Sewanee to New York: you are a party in a box and I will always love and cherish your friendship. Jamie—thank you for always being ready with hours of Top 40 hits and the never-to-be-forgotten (and never-to-be-repeated) Kyle Chandler dinner. Katherine—thank you for just being you and for the years of laughter about your antics and stories. Kitty and Janie—how is possible that you still look the same as you did our first days of college? Our visits are never long enough. Libba—thank you for your amazing support.

As a child, I can still remember the soft hands of our nanny, Miss Sellers, who filled our days with Bible verses and always reminded me that true beauty is on the inside. I know that you are watching over me from heaven, Miss Sellers.

I have been so fortunate to have such a wonderful support system in my own home with Rhea Marasigan. My children are so lucky to have your loving presence in their lives. Thank you for loving our children like your own.

It is hard to believe that it was five years ago that I sat across the table from Jason Weinberg, Uma Thurman, and Gabrielle Kachman as we discussed "what to do with my talent." Thank you three for a delicious breakfast and a conversation that gave me the confidence to set this book in motion.

A massive thank-you to Keith Fox, who handed over his

Rolodex of business contacts to help me understand what it takes to write a book and supported me along the way. Looking forward to many more breakfasts in the years to come.

And then there is Meg. Agent extraordinaire. Thank you for believing in me, supporting me, and getting this proposal into the hands of the extraordinary Simon & Schuster team. Your honesty and wisdom gave me the confidence to find my voice and write this book. How has this happened in a year? And a huge thank-you for the keen editorial eye of Cindy Uh, who is not only an incredibly talented agent, but also one in whom I see a kindred cheerleading spirit. Thank you for your wisdom and your unwavering support in this process.

But an agent has to have someone who sees potential in a book and wants to help craft it into a story that will make it a bestseller (no pressure here!). Cara Bedick, how can I ever thank you for enough for your genius instinct? Thank you for taking such incredible care of this book from the first edits to the final edits. It is a book that I will always be proud to read. You are an amazing editor, and an incredible woman.

To Susan, Tara, Meredith, Shida, and the rest of the incredible Touchstone team. You had me at hello. Though we won't end the journey together, you will always be my first book-writing family. To Jen, Karyn, and the Gallery team, who understood my vision for this book and helped me knock it out of the park. Thank you all for your incredible support and amazing instincts from our first meeting. This is just the beginning!

Simon & Schuster—I have been living on top of my dream for twenty years. I am so honored to be publishing my first book with your house.

To Megan Salt. You are a ROCK STAR. I am so proud to be

your friend and one of the first DSRC clients. How can I ever re-pay you for your spot-on advice and incredible work ethic? Julia Ruttner, Sunil Desai, and Daniel Gabbay, I am so lucky to have you on my team. You have all worked tirelessly to bring this book to the world. I cannot thank you enough for your advice and guidance.

I have spent the past twenty years walking in the front door of Christie's Auction House in Rockefeller Plaza, surrounded by the best and brightest talent in the world.

In a mountain of thank-yous, the first one goes to Mary Libby, who picked up the phone day after day in 1998, and gave me the chance of a lifetime.

When entering a company at such a young age, the wisdom and leadership of the person who runs your department sets the tone for your managerial style for the rest of your life. Lauren Shortt, you were an amazing role model and, above all, friend. You included me in every opportunity at work and even filled my weekends with your plans. Thank you for your kindness. From my beginning years working late nights as the happiest intern in the world with Jen Ketron, Nicole Garwood, Nathalie Kaplan, and Robert Swingle to securing my first job in special events where I met my first Christie's/New York friends, Lindsey Rogers, Monica Eulitz, and Allison Comer, every day was more fun than the last. Visse Wedell—I learned more from you both personally and pro-fessionally than you will ever know. You are a true original.

Morgan Tupper and Maggie Borner—those insane, intense years running events will forever remain some of my favorite times at Christie's. Even after twelve hours in the office, we never wanted to leave one another at the end of the night. I would happily spend twelve hours with you two any day of the week. It's fair to say that our surprise mechanical bull at the staff party is legend. Mags—thanks for the long swims, the longer talks, and your loyal friendship all of these years.

Every team and every year that has followed has brought such amazing memories—Adrianna Archer, Jane Shull, Sue Bohlen, Kendall Moore, Sydney LaLonde, Caroline Spencer, Christina Starr, Jess Baca, Anne Prentnieks, Nikole Yurt, Rebecca Barden, Katrina Yap: thank you for making the office a place that felt like home.

Who could ever forget my boss, but more like my work husband, George McNeely, who spent the first few years of my job trying to find a prince for me. You are the best dance partner, wedding toast giver, friend, and work husband around. Our trips to Brazil were some of the best trips of my life.

And to my travel partner in crime, Mariana Wall, whose laugh shakes the walls and in whom I found another sister. May your passport always be fully stamped. You are an extraordinary woman—thank you for your unwavering support all of these years.

To Lauren Land, for your hilarious sense of humor, your ability to tell it like it is, and your indomitable spirit. I am so proud of everything that you have accomplished, and so proud of the amazing woman that you have become.

To Toby, who taught me to never ask for permission, only for forgiveness. Your ability to pursue what you believe is right is beyond inspiring. Creating the Green Auction with you will stand as one of the most stressful and rewarding times in my career. To the future success of FU. A special thanks to Harlan for always being my underbidder.

To Amy Wexler, for everything. I am so impressed by your wise counsel, your thoughtfulness, and your tiger-momness. The sky is the limit for you and I hope you know I am here to support you in your ascent.

To the rest of my Christie's family—Marc Porter, Stephen Lash, Jonathan Rendell, Jen Zatorski, Maria Los, Jen Hall, Heather Barnhart, Ellanor Notides, Capera Ryan, Lydia Kimball, Stacey Sayer, Marissa Wilcox, Julie Kim, Sheri Farber, Caroline Sayan, Jen Wright, Tash Perrin, Bonnie Brennan, Karen Gray, Erin McAndrew, Sara Fox, Becca Riegelhaupt, Sayuri Ganepola, Lolita Persaud, Marcia Davis, Steve Zick, Cathy Busch, Lucy Campbell, Alex Reid, Sara Friedlander, Alexis Klein, Helen Cousar, Lilly Robicsek, Michael Moore, John Hays, Jody Wilkie, Virgilio Garza, Margot Rosenberg, Bliss Summers, Cat Manson, Lola Martins, Alexandra Jaffray, Robbie Gordy, Kristin Kolich, Jessica Katz, Kathy Coumou, Bennett Jackson, Arianna Savage, Christopher Burge, and Steve Wrightson. I grew up with many of you, and have spent half of my life as part of the Christie's team. I am continually awed and inspired by everything you do. I am so proud to call you colleagues and friends.

Lexy, Lily, Suus, Alexi, and Claudia. There are no words to thank you for your constant support and encouragement throughout this entire process. You were there through the highs and lows with amazing advice, positive attitudes, and a willingness to help brainstorm or simply let me talk every step of the way. I am the luckiest woman in the world to work with you every day. Welcome to the department, Poppy! We have loved you since the minute you were born.

To my fellow charity auctioneers—your dedication to raising money for nonprofits after-hours when everyone else has long since left the office is incredible. Keep rocking the stage.

To my New York friends, who have become family over the last twenty years.

And to my friends, who are my family.

Alex Buckley, whose friendship I found on long beach walks in

Amagansett and the ski slopes of St. Anton. Thank you for your words of wisdom, your friendship, and your willingness to dive DEEP into any topic on a moment's notice. A special thanks for your introduction to the insanely talented Gemma Burgess, whose advice and beautiful mastery of the English language helped me create the title for this book.

Courtney Smith—Have we started a movement? I admire you more every day that I spend with you. You are a force in the world and I am so proud to be your friend.

Kate Schelter, who told me to WRITE THIS BOOK in no uncertain terms over a pint of Seven Seas ice cream in Cape Cod. Your honesty is something to behold. Your words stay with me. I can't wait to see the new heights that you will reach in the coming years.

Some of the greatest gifts I have received from my marriage to Chris are the friendships from Apt. 4C. Heidi Allen—I admire your strength, determination, and unwavering commitment to your faith and family. I will never forget our conversation on the Cape. This book is for the girls who become who they are despite what people told them. Geoff Allen—you are another brother to me and the only person I know who likes to talk as much as I do. We are so lucky to have you both in our lives. And to the other third of our original family from 4C. Erin Forker—the introduction to this book was written in your car after we finished our spin class this summer. Thank you for the swims across Hamblin Pond. Rob Forker—thank you for your candor in our conversations, and your great business advice. Even though you didn't live in 4C, you will always be part of the family, Andrew and Kristin Wessel. Andrew—thank you for showing me what negotiation can look like without any scruples. Kristin—looking forward to many more trips to the lake.

To Darren and Sara MacDonald—the best neighbors and friends

we could have hoped for in New York. Thank you for allowing our children into your home (or is it their home?) and your readiness for a conversation, advice, or a glass of wine any day of the week.

How could I have known that preschool would be so much fun? For me? To my Tribeca mom squad—I love each of you so much. Little K/Karina Heffers, Therese Lundqvist, Alex Frankel, and Lindsey Goldfaden—pickup and drop-off were the best part of my days during the preschool years at Washington Market because of each of you. You are such amazing women, true friends, and the creators of quite a few epic NYC nights. If I could laugh as hard as I did the night that Little K lit up the stage at El Toucan, my life would be complete. I look forward to many more nights in the years to come.

And to my friends who created a place of respite for our family outside of New York City. Caitlin and Mick Davis—for so many laughs, incredible stories, delicious bottles of wine, and years of friendship. As long as you keep the ghosts away, we will always come to stay.

Ashley and Davin Staats, whose three-course meals make a weekend away seem more like a hotel stay than a quick trip outside of the city. Ash—thank you for the long conversations, the nonstop exercise, and the solid Midwestern advice that roots you and makes you the real deal.

To the incredible women who I have come to know and love over the past twenty years. I consider you New Yorkers either because we met here or because you are a New Yorker at heart:

Cena Jackson, Sara Gilbane, Tiffin Jernstedt, Sloan Overstrom, Morgan Hutchinson, Beth McCann, Kristin Henderson, Brooke Lampley, Danielle Snyder, Jodie Snyder, Jenny Rothenberg, Ellin Delsener, Camilla Andersson, Joann Pailey, Alex Muldoon, Allison O'Neill, Whitney Vargas, Hilary Neve, Jackie Seaman, Katie Radford, Amy Pasquariello, Maggie Smith, Rachelle Hruska MacPherson,

Amory McAndrew, Lauren Silverman, Jenna Hager, Annelise Winters, Coralie Charriol Paul, Jackie Dimitri, Jenny Vorhoff, Catherine Juracich, Grace Cha, Amy Haklisch, Bergin O'Malley, Brooke Fisch, Meghan Rogers, and Phoebe Polk.

To my surrogate little sister, Ashley Venetos, for her incredible, wise-beyond-her-years advice, her kind heart, and for always being a wonderful friend to Hilary and the Fenet family.

A special thanks to the guys in my life who seem more like brothers than friends: Andrew Wessel, Jamie Dimitri, John McCann, Grove Stafford, John Heffers, Jeff Goldfaden, Henrik Lundqvist, Bronson van Wyck, Josh Wood, Britt Rogers, and Grant Frankel. Brian Haklisch—thank you for taking such amazing photos and letting me ride your electric skateboard despite the ridicule from CBD.

A million thanks for the words of wisdom to all the amazing women who contributed stories and advice to this book. You are the role models for our future leaders. There are no words to thank you enough: Holly Dunlap, Meghan O'Leary, Mia Kang, Martha Stewart, Gemma Burgess, Kate Harbin Clammer, Noria Morales, Barbara Corcoran, Deborah Roberts, Mary Alice Stephenson, Dee Poku, Alexandra Lebenthal, Ashley Miles, Tiffin Jernstedt, Julia Taylor Cheek, Alexandra Wilkis Wilson, Lauren Brody, Kristen Morrissey Thiede, Meena Harris, Karen Spencer, Morgan Hutchinson, Emilie Rubinfeld, Catherine Hernandez-Blades, Nina Garcia, Linda Guerrero, Alexandra Buckley Voris, Mary Giuliani, Bettina Prentice, Sarah Kate Ellis, Courtney Smith, Kate Schelter, and Sian Beilock. I am so honored that you included your hard-earned advice in this book. I know that the readers will benefit from reading your lessons as much as I did. Thank you from the bottom of my heart.

Thank you for watching over me from heaven, Pawpaw, Grandpa, and Granny.

And finally, although you aren't here to read this book, Maman, I hope you know that you taught me what it means to be a steel magnolia. The memories of driving to the country club in your Cadillac after church on Sunday will stay with me forever. You are with me always.

ABOUT THE AUTHOR

Lydia Fenet has raised more than half a billion dollars for non-profits and charitable organizations as one of the top auctioneers in the world. She is often found on stage alongside high-profile executives and celebrities. Lydia built and oversees the strategic partnerships department at Christie's, the world's leading auction house, where she serves as a senior vice president. In addition to her role within Christie's, she travels internationally to train corporations and groups on topics including empowering women in the workplace, mastering public speaking, and motivating your sales force. Lydia's auctioneering achievements have been featured in the *New York Times*, the *Wall Street Journal*, *Forbes*, *Vogue*, *Crain's*, *Elle*, *Vanity Fair*, and more. Lydia lives in New York City with her husband and three children.